LOAVES
and
FISHES

*But Jesus said to them: They have no need to go. Give you them to eat.
They answered him: We have not here but five loaves and two fishes.
He said to them: Bring them hither to me.*

*And, when he had commanded the multitudes to sit down upon the
grass, he took the five loaves and the two fishes; and looking up to heaven,
he blessed and brake and gave the loaves to his disciples, and the disciples
to the multitudes.*

And they did all eat and were filled. . . .   Matthew 14:16-20

LOAVES

and

FISHES

DOROTHY DAY

Introduction by Robert Coles

1817

HARPER & ROW, PUBLISHERS, San Francisco
Cambridge, Hagerstown, New York, Philadelphia
London, Mexico City, São Paulo, Sydney

Frontispiece: After the noon meal at the Chrystie Street House of Hospitality, a few guests linger over a second cup of coffee, while latecomers hope there is still some soup left. Meanwhile, the staff prepares for supper.

LOAVES AND FISHES
Copyright © 1963 by Dorothy Day.
Introduction copyright © 1983 by Robert Coles.
All rights reserved. Printed in the United States of America. No part of this book may be used or reproduced in any manner whatsoever without written permission except in the case of brief quotations embodied in critical articles and reviews. For information address Harper & Row, Publishers, Inc., 10 East 53rd Street, New York, NY 10022. Published simultaneously in Canada by Fitzhenry & Whiteside, Limited, Toronto.

FIRST HARPER & ROW PAPERBACK EDITION PUBLISHED IN 1983.

Library of Congress Cataloging in Publication Data

Day, Dorothy, 1897–1981
  LOAVES AND FISHES.

  1. Day, Dorothy, 1897–1981   2. Catholics—United States—Biography.   3. Catholic worker.   4. Catholic Worker Movement.
I. Title.
BX4705.D283A35   1983   267'.182'0924 [B]   82-48433
ISBN 0-06-061771-3

83 84 85 86 87 10 9 8 7 6 5 4 3 2 1

Contents

Introduction by Robert Coles   vii

Preface   xiii

Part I. Beginnings Are Always Exciting

1. A Knock at the Door   3
2. Everyone's Paper   12
3. Houses of Hospitality   28
4. Communitarian Farms   42
5. The War Years   60

Part II. Poverty and Precarity

6. The Faces of Poverty   67
7. The Insulted and the Injured   71
8. A Baby Is Always Born with a Loaf of Bread
   Under Its Arm   78

Part III. Those Who Work Together

9. Peter Maurin, Personalist   93
10. Picture of a Prophet   103
11. Spiritual Advisors   118
12. Editors Also Cook   131

Part IV. Things That Happen

13. What Has Become of Anna? 149
14. The Bodenheims 151
15. Strange Visitors, Distinguished Visitors 156
16. The "Cold Turkey" Cure 160

Part V. Love in Practice

17. A Block Off the Bowery 181
18. Peter Maurin Farm 194
19. Our Day 205
Acknowledgments 216

Introduction

by Robert Coles

I SUPPOSE WE MIGHT WELL CALL IT THE CATHOLIC WORKER MOVEMENT, that effort initiated in the early 1930s by Peter Maurin and Dorothy Day; but neither of them would have especially appreciated such a description. They saw themselves as struggling, penitent Christians, anxious to connect the religious pieties so many of us collect (as if quaint cultural heirlooms) to the concrete moral challenges of everyday life. Put differently, they could not get out of their minds, day after day, the example Jesus set as he walked the Galilee of two thousand years ago, not only encouraging, admonishing, exhorting, explaining, summoning, but time and again, doing. As He moved from town to town He saw what is visible for anyone, anywhere, anytime—the hurt and anguish and suffering of human beings. He saw the hungry, the thirsty, and He moved to give them food, drink. He saw the lame, the blind, and He moved to heal them. He saw the outcast, the scorned, the despised, the utterly lowly, the defenseless, and He was moved to affirm their worth, their dignity. And, too, He saw the powerful, the ever-so-important, the self-righteous, and He turned on them with a stunning vehemence: they may be among the highest, the first in this worldly life, but their future is by no means secure—indeed, they may be in the greatest of jeopardy *sub specie aeternitatis*.

Nor was Jesus loath to live as He urged others to live. He not only requested a commitment to love others, He revealed a readiness to embrace without qualification the very sad and vulnerable people whom He met—not only help them, teach them, but take up their lives. Nor did He do so in a self-important or hectoring way. He was unwilling to replace one kind of arrogance with another. No one has a right, He reminded His listeners—He reminded all of us—to assume the posture of the accuser, the finger-pointing moralist, hungry for a target of condemnation, without having first engaged in the closest of self-scrutiny. And so doing, what criteria ought we summon? Why, only those "without sin" (and therefore, none of us) have the right to "cast stones," make invidious and smug remarks about others.

No wonder, with such a moral example, Dorothy Day and Peter Maurin shunned the world of big, important people in favor of the down-and-out of New York City. No wonder they never tried to turn their efforts, and those of the hundreds and hundreds who eventually joined hands with them, into yet another political, social or intellectual "movement"—hence the difficulty one has in using words to describe what they have done, what continues to be done all over the United States. Maybe we should settle for one verbal approximation Dorothy Day made—though hardly of the kind to earn her and her kindred souls credit in twentieth-century America's marketplace of ideas: "fools for Christ."

The Son of God most certainly did offer us a topsy-turvy vision of things, and to this day the result has been a response of outright rejection, nervous indifference, and maybe worst of all, the eager ingratiation that characterizes pietism—form without substance. More than anything, those men and women who have become Catholic Workers—meaning, imbued with a sense of things inspired by Dorothy Day and Peter Maurin—have wanted to fight such responses. To do so, they realized, would require deeds, not words, however fresh, earnest, and appealing. To do so, really, would require the assumption of a kind of *life* as well as a point of view—religious faith not only espoused but lived.

This book of Dorothy Day's tries to give an account of what such a life has meant. The wonderful irony is that her words are doubly redeemed—they are an afterword, of sorts, to many years of hard labor, and they are as direct and simple and unpretentious and earnest and strongly felt as that labor was meant to be. In *The Long*

Loneliness Miss Day told us about her own personal pilgrimage; and there are now in print biographical accounts of both her life and that of Peter Maurin. *Loaves and Fishes* renders us the reason those books are of continuing interest: a territory of Christian concern was staked out and settled with love—and so the explorers deserve our somewhat awed respect. We may never, many of us, be able to work in New York City's Bowery as is done, right now, by members of the Catholic Worker community, but we have an obligation to ourselves to know what it is possible for our fellow human beings to imagine, and more important, to bring into being, to realize, day in, day out.

No question, Dorothy Day was a marvelously able journalist and essayist. Her writing has always been lean, sturdy, quietly persuasive. She is at her best here—at once reflective, anecdotal, suggestive, and in her own way, bluntly analytical. That last quality ought to be emphasized, I believe, at this particular moment, because now that Dorothy Day is gone (she died late in 1981, at the age of 83) all too many of us will be tempted to romanticize her life and wrap her various exertions of body and spirit, of heart, mind, and soul, with a thick covering of sugary sentiment—a means of dismissal, a burial for our convenience of what actually is still very much alive, as anyone who visits the Catholic Worker communities in, say, Los Angeles or Boston or Washington, D.C., and elsewhere across the nation will readily observe.

Throughout the following pages the author is at pains to tell us what happens, as these works of Christian mercy are done: the everyday attention paid the hungry, the sick, the destitute, the badly confused, the repeatedly victimized ones of our particular industrial society. She also wants us to understand not only the biblical roots of this singular endeavor, but the modern resonances—the anarchist politics, the personalist philosophy, the literary and moral sensibility of Dostoevski and Tolstoy, of Dickens, even (at least in part) of J. D. Salinger and Camus. She was, to be sure, loyal to the Catholic Church and to a certain version of American populism; but her true loyalty was to the communitarian fellowship of the early Christians. That is to say, she had little regard for three major loyalties, if not social passions, of our time: nationalism, materialism, the self. She and others like her have seen only too clearly how much, alas, capitalists and communists, the well-to-do and the aspiring members of this "proletariat" or that "bourgeoisie" manage to share, with respect to ideas and ideals, hopes and worries. Christ's radical call is bound to make all who heed it "alienated," she knew—and for having come to that condition, she also knew, one can only be grateful. One can only contrast such an insistently iconoclastic attitude toward this world's prevailing assumptions with the beliefs and opinions most of us hold and, as a matter of fact, aim to hold.

Very important, also, is the persistent self-criticism one encounters in these pages—a contrast, surely, with the ideological mind we of this century have found to be so prevalent. "It takes some time," Miss Day says at one point, near the end of her narrative, "to calm one's heart, which fills all too easily with irritation, resentment, and anger." A bit further on, with no suspicious show of self-loathing aimed at deflecting criticism, but rather in a terse moment of candor, she remarks upon some of the hurdles and obstacles of fate and circumstance faced by others, then observes this about her own tasks: "How little we have attempted, let alone accomplished."

One quickly disagrees, yet is somehow touched by an edifying inclination to play down, rather than up, the character of a particular community's purposes. More personally, she offers us moments such as this: "It was my interior fear and harshness that I was judging in myself." Not that (thank God!) this twentieth-century writer and activist is addicted to a version of the besetting sin of pride which, these days, takes the form of an endless, self-centered psychological examination. She ridicules an "analyzing and introspection and examination of conscience" which take place in the abstract (unconnected to specific ethical responsibilities) or which are done *ex post facto*—meaning, so often, *after* any risk or danger or sacrifice is at issue. If she is all too aware, though, of her "failures in love," of her "neglects," her "falls," she is equally mindful that under no conditions ought those lapses, inevitable in all of us, be made an excuse for yet additional sins: a resignation or a despair that justifies, of course, apathy or a turning away from a given course of action.

This book is not to be read in the expectation of a linear argument, or in hopes of obtaining an "agenda" of one sort or another. Dorothy Day as a writer offers the challenge (and pleasure) of a marvelously complex mind. She does not shirk the ironies and ambiguities, if not outright paradoxes or contradictions or inconsistencies, which her way of thinking inevitably generates. "I condemn poverty," she says when she takes up the subject in Chapter 6, "and I advocate it." She immediately, of course, wants to help the reader comprehend this way of reasoning; she distinguishes between poverty as a "social phenomenon" and poverty as "a personal matter." She abhorred the poverty she saw in the tenements of our cities—men, women, children in dire straits because there is no work, because the work they have pays little, because society chooses to ignore their predicament. But she also took care to notice the stinginess and mean-spirited greed which are not rarely associated with wealth and power. She wanted no part of all that—the crass commercialism, the acquisitiveness which by no means disappear with an ample and well-diversified stock portfolio. Christ had urged her kind of poverty on His Disciples, and she urged it on herself: a poverty that stresses generosity to others and an unflagging personal dedication to the requirements of social justice.

There are rewards in such a life. They are not those many of us have come to anticipate or expect, but they must certainly be mentioned. Over and over Dorothy Day lets us know that for her the satisfactions of a given (and freely chosen) life have been large, indeed. She and her co-workers, after all, have themselves been in need; in feeding and clothing others they have tried to find a measure of self-respecting intimacy with their religious faith. Again an irony: out of one's own jeopardy (in the eyes of God, not Mammon) one responds to the jeopardy of others. Christ's parables, His shrewd and terribly demanding analogies, similes, metaphors, in their sum, instruct and warn us, but also point in a direction—one

Loaves and Fishes documents, one taken freely by some of our fellow citizens in this century's America. We in this country have been blessed in many ways by nature and history. We have also been blessed, one dares think, by God Himself—not in the all-too-banal sense of "God Bless America," but in the concrete sense of a rare and especially honorable life given us, that of a Christian pilgrim. Her body is gone, yes, but her soul presses close upon us still: in the "works" she helped inspire, which continue to grace us, and no less in her words, so luminous and passionate, so wedded to those of Christ Himself, as in *Loaves and Fishes*.

Preface

THIS BOOK IS THE STORY OF *The Catholic Worker*, A STORY I ONLY touched on in my autobiography, *The Long Loneliness*, published some years ago. What is *The Catholic Worker?* First of all, it is an eight-page monthly tabloid paper. The writing in it concerns work and men and the problems of poverty and destitution—and man's relationship to his brothers and to God. In trying to show our love for our brothers, we talk and write a great deal about works of mercy, as the most direct form of action. "Direct action" is a slogan of old-time radicals. In the thirties it meant bringing ideas to the man in the street via picketing and leaflets, storming employment offices, marching on Washington. Today, in the peace movement, direct action means boarding Polaris submarines, walking to Moscow, and sailing boats like *The Everyman* into areas where nuclear testing is going on.

Peter Maurin, co-founder of *The Catholic Worker*, insisted that the works of mercy are the most direct form of action there is. "But the truth needs to be restated every twenty years," he said.

Works of mercy are feeding the hungry, giving drink to the thirsty, clothing the naked, sheltering the homeless, visiting the sick, ransoming the prisoner, and burying the dead. The spiritual works of mercy are instructing the ignorant, counseling the doubtful, rebuking the sinner, bearing wrongs patiently, forgiving all injuries, and praying for the living and the dead.

Writing about these things, we have also to try to practice them. Readers come to us with their difficulties and we have to give what immediate aid we can. Also, in the last few years we have been more and more concerned with world peace—or rather with the threats to peace and to the very survival of mankind.

What kind of an organization do we have? It's hard to answer that. We don't have any, in the usual sense of the word. Certainly we are not a cooperative, not a settlement house, not a mission. We cannot be said to operate on a democratic basis. Once both an ex-soldier and an ex-Trappist were staying with us, and I asked each in turn how he liked The Catholic Worker group. The soldier said, "It's just like the Army," and the Trappist said, "It's like a Trappist monastery." Then a man from an Israeli *kibbutz* visited us and I asked him the same question. He felt very much at home, he said, because the atmosphere was that of the *kibbutzim*. A visitor from India likened our city house of hospitality to an *ashram*. A teacher of Russian at Fordham told us our farming commune reminded her of Tolstoi's home. Someone else called it a benevolent dictatorship.

Perhaps the most accurate description was supplied by the friend who referred to it as a "revolutionary headquarters."

Young people in particular have always liked the word "revolution" because it implies action, change, the renewed struggle for a better world. This is one reason why The Catholic Worker attracts so many young people. Picketing, distributing literature that provokes thought and argument—such activities as these offer exciting outlets for principles in action; and the fact that the editors have been in jail many times for civil disobedience makes our work seem dangerous and therefore more challenging and attractive. More and more, young people see in our work the opportunity they seek to act directly against the threat of nuclear war.

Perhaps it is only through reading of our growth and struggles over the years, through coming to know those who have shaped our movement and given substance to our thought, that you can truly grasp what we stand for, what we are trying to achieve. This is why I am writing the story of The Catholic Worker.

As the palmist of old sang at the dawn of a new day, "Now I have begun."

Part I

Beginnings
Are Always Exciting

< *Hostile or friendly, Union Square habitués*
were curious enough about a Catholic
radical paper in 1933 to read it.

Chapter 1

A Knock at the Door

IT IS A JOY TO ME TO SIT IN FRONT OF A WINDOW AND WRITE IN this way, in my little two-room apartment on Ludlow Street. This is in an old slum section of New York (the Lower East Side) which is not yet being boarded up or demolished.

The day is very hot, but my windows, facing east, look out on a back yard with a bare tree, an ailanthus tree—the tree of heaven. Down in the next yard are a maple and some bushes.

The sun pours in on the rooms, which are freshly painted. Next door, two other rooms face onto the yard. In these four rooms there are at present five of us: besides me, a girl just out of prison; a seventeen-year-old schoolgirl, a runaway; a serious young college student of twenty-one whose commitment to the intellectual life means her ideas may overflow into action; and a girl on vacation from a hospital for the poor in Montreal, where she gives her services to the crippled and the destitute.

Yes, it is a joy to write in these surroundings. But it is a confinement, too: the ailanthus tree, bare though it may be, yet reaches up bonily in this New York canyon of back yards for a bit of air and sunlight.

My mind goes back. I am reminded of an apartment much like this one, four rooms deep, at East Fifteenth Street and Avenue A, where I was living when I started *The Catholic Worker* with Peter Maurin. All those old houses are torn down now, but there was a row of them then along the narrow street, occupied mostly by Germans and Italians.

I was living with my younger brother, John, and Teresa, his Spanish wife. Our kitchen looked out on a back yard where there were no ailanthuses—that tough weed of a tree—but fig trees, carefully cultivated and guarded by Italians, who corseted them in hay and burlap against the cold during the winter. In the summer the trees bore fruit. There were peach trees, privet hedges growing as high as trees, and rows of widow's-tears. Petunias and marigolds gave us a small riot of color—and delightful fragrance, too, whenever the rain washed the air clear of the neighborhood cooking smells.

We were in the third year of the depression. Roosevelt had just been elected President. Every fifth adult American—twelve million in all—was unemployed. No smoke came from the factories. Mortgages on homes and farms were being foreclosed, driving more people to the city and loading them onto the already overburdened relief rolls. In New York long, bedraggled breadlines of listless men wound along city streets. On the fringes, by the rivers, almost every vacant lot was a Hooverville, a collection of jerry-built shanties where the homeless huddled in front of their fires.

An air of excitement, of impending social change, with the opportunity to implement our social ideas, buoyed up all who were young and had ideas. We met, we talked endlessly, feeling that this was the time to try new things. I had just come back from Washington, where I was covering the story of the Hunger March of the Unemployed Councils for *Commonweal* and the story of the Farmers' Conference for *America*. I had been a journalist most of my days, and I was earning my living by freelance writing of articles about the social order.

Sitting in the kitchen one afternoon, I was working on a book about the unemployed—it was to be a novel—when a knock came at the door. Tessa was just starting supper. John was getting ready to go to work—he was a copy boy on a Hearst paper at the time. They were both twenty years old and expecting their first baby. Tessa had a warm, radiant look, a glowing look. John was more reserved.

Tessa, who was always very hospitable, welcomed the man at

the door. A short, broad man (he was fifty-seven, I found out later, but my first impression was that he was older) came in and started talking at once—casually, informally, almost as though he were taking up a conversation where it had been left off. There was a gray look about him: he had gray hair, cut short and scrubby; gray eyes; strong features; a pleasant mouth; and short-fingered, broad hands, evidently used to heavy work, such as with a pick and shovel. He wore the kind of old clothes that have so lost their shape and finish that it's impossible to tell whether they are clean or not. But Peter Maurin, agitator and soon to be founder of what came to be known as The Catholic Worker movement, was, as I later learned, always neat.

Tessa went on with her work and the newcomer stood before me, declaiming one of what John named his "Easy Essays":

> People go to Washington
> asking the government
> to solve their economic problems,
> while the Federal government
> was never intended
> to solve men's economic problems.
> Thomas Jefferson says that
> the less government there is
> the better it is.
> If the less government there is,
> the better it is,
> then the best kind of government
> is self-government.
> If the best kind of government
> is self-government,
> then the best kind of organization
> is self-organization.
>
> When the organizers try
> to organize the unorganized,
> then the organizers
> don't organize themselves.
> And when the organizers
> don't organize themselves,
> nobody organizes himself,
> and when nobody organizes himself
> nothing is organized.

Dorothy Day and her daughter, Tamar, in the early 1930's.

He actually spoke this way, using repetition to make his points. He phrased these points so simply that they sounded like free verse (and to this day people talk about "Peter's verses").

Tamar, my little daughter, had been calling me from the next room. She was down with measles, and she wanted orange juice and me. For his part, Peter wanted a listener and a disciple, so he went on talking to a doctor who had just come in. When the doctor left, he talked to the plumber, to the gasman reading the meter, to Tessa at the kitchen sink, and to John, while he was shaving before the kitchen mirror.

I learned from Tessa that he had actually come to see me. Tessa had a wonderful serenity, but I felt torn apart. The doctor, Tamar, and Peter all wanted my undivided attention at this moment, and I was dulled by my own fatigue as well. Peter had come a few times before to see if I was back from Washington, and Tessa had welcomed him; but John, solid American that he was, had not been so sure whether Peter was someone I would want to see or a crackpot from Union Square. Peter had told Tessa—his French accent made him hard to understand at first—that he had read articles I wrote in Catholic magazines and had come to suggest I start a newspaper to bring about "clarification of thought." Clarification was the first "point" in his program. Men must think before they act. They must study. "There could be no revolution without a theory of revolution," he had quoted Lenin as saying, and what he himself was interested in was the "green revolution," the back-to-the-land revolution, not the red one, which emphasized industry. It was because I had just come back from Washington that he had delivered to me his "People go to Washington" essay, but in my mixed roles as cook, dishwasher, nurse, and mother, as well as writer, it was hard for me to grasp what he said immediately.

It was a long time before I really knew what Peter was talking about that first day. But he did make three points I thought I understood: founding a newspaper for clarification of thought, starting houses of hospitality, and organizing farming communes. I did not really think then of the latter two as having anything to do with me, but I did know about newspapers. My father and three brothers worked on them all their adult lives. When I was eleven, we children had started to type out a little family newspaper. We all liked to write, and I had been taught early to write personally, subjectively, about what I saw around me and what was being done.

Tamar was not very sick. She was content for a few days to play with dolls and kittens and modeling clay, and Peter took advantage of my confinement at home to come back and continue my indoctrination.

"He who is not a Socialist at twenty has no heart, and he who is a Socialist at thirty has no head," he was fond of quoting from a French author. Since I had been a Socialist in college, a Communist in the early twenties, and now a Catholic since 1927, I had a very definite point of view about poverty, unemployment, and my own vocation to try to do something about it all. I had no doubts about the Church. It was founded upon Saint Peter, that rock, who yet thrice denied his Master on the eve of His crucifixion. And Jesus had compared the Church to a net cast into the sea and hauled in, filled with fishes, both good and bad. "Including," one of my non-Catholic friends used to say, "some blowfish and quite a few sharks."

Peter Maurin spoke to me often of his ideas about hospitality, a concept I understood well because I had lived so long on the Lower East Side of New York—and the poor are noted for their hospitality. "There is always enough for one more," my brother's Spanish mother-in-law used to say. "Everyone just take a little less." Poor families were always taking in other needy ones. So, when Peter began talking about what "we need," it sounded clear and logical:

> The Catholic unemployed
> should not be sent to the Muni
>   [municipal lodging house].
> The Catholic unemployed
> should be given hospitality
> in Catholic Houses of Hospitality.
> Catholic Houses of Hospitality
> are known in Europe
> under the name of hospices.
> There have been hospices in Europe
> since the time of Constantine.
> Hospices are free guest houses;
> hotels are paying guest houses.
> And paying guest houses or hospices
> are as plentiful
> as free guest houses or hospices
> are scarce.
> So hospitality, like everything else
> has been commercialized.

So hospitality, like everything else,
must now be idealized.

Some of Peter's other ideas were less readily understandable, but his verses probably helped people grasp the sense and spirit of what he had to say. He fancied himself a troubadour of God, going about the public squares and street corners indoctrinating his listeners by a singsong repetition, which certainly caught their attention. Being a born teacher, he did not hesitate to repeat his ideas over and over again. He even suggested to the young students and unemployed who flocked around him and accompanied him to Columbus Circle that there should be a sort of antiphonal chant. Peter would sing out, "To give and not to take," and the chorus would respond, "That is what makes man human," and so on, through the entire essay.

He was good as bread. He was not gay or joyful, as others have described him, but he was a truly happy man, with the happiness a man feels when he has found his vocation in life and has set out on the way and is sure of himself: and sure, too, that others are searching for and willing to undertake their task in life, striving not only to love God and their brother but to *show* that love. Peter had faith in people as well as in ideas, and he was able to make them feel his faith in them, so that they gained confidence and overcame the sense of futility that so plagues the youth of today. In fact, he gave me so great a faith in the power of his ideas that if he had said, "Go to Madison Square Garden and speak these ideas," I would have overcome all sense of fear and would have attempted such a folly, convinced that, though it was the "folly of the Cross" and doomed to failure, God Himself could take this failure and turn it into victory.

Certainly there was nothing in Peter's physical appearance to impress his hearers. His dusty, unpressed, ill-fitting suit bulged with books and pamphlets; yet he gave no impression of carelessness, for he invariably wore a felt hat (not too wide-brimmed), a shirt (rough-dried), a tie, and sturdy shoes. He was not the bearded, sandaled, hatless fanatic—he had no appearance of an apostle. Neither was he establishing a personality cult; it was the primacy of the spiritual that Peter always emphasized. He was

The date and place of this picture are unknown, but Peter Maurin's spectacles were, as usual, askew.

happy when people listened to him, yet he did not want people to follow him because of the influence he himself exerted but only because of the strength and beauty of the idea.

The idea of poverty, for instance. How glowing a thing it is in Franciscan literature, and how many illusions people have about it! But Peter *lived* it. He literally possessed nothing. He lived in an old hotel on the Bowery where he paid fifty cents a night for his lodging. He ate, when he had the money, in the "horse markets" of the Bowery, cheap cafés serving stew and hot weak coffee, very sweet. He was used to living on soup and bread.

Among his ideas it was the one of publishing a paper which most immediately appealed to me. "But how can it be done without money?" I wanted to know.

"In the Catholic Church one never needs any money to start a good work," Peter replied. "People are what are important. If you have the people and they are willing to give their work— that is the thing. God is not to be outdone in generosity. The funds will come in somehow or other."

Did he really say this? I cannot be sure now, and I suspect that he passed over my question about money—it was not needed in the Church. The important thing was work.

I had been reading the life of Rose Hawthorne Lathrop. She

was a daughter of Nathaniel Hawthorne, the nineteenth-century American novelist. Rose, with her husband, had become a convert in 1891. She had started a cancer hospital for the poor and homeless—such institutions were a rarity in those days—in three dark, airless rooms down on the East Side. Her beginnings had been as humble as ours would be if I started the work Peter wanted. Indeed, when Rose herself fell ill with grippe, her very first patient had to take care of her. But from that simple start her work had grown until there are now a half dozen of those hospitals, run by the Dominicans, scattered around the country. A new order of nuns, wearing the Dominican habit, came into being as a result.

Reading about Rose Hawthorne Lathrop and listening now to Peter so inspired me that I was quite ready to believe that in the Church no money was necessary. I was all for plunging right in. After all, I had a typewriter and a kitchen table and plenty of paper and plenty to write about. The thing was to find a printer, run off the first issue and go out on the streets and sell it. Beginnings are always exciting.

Chapter 2

Everyone's Paper

SOMEONE ONCE SAID THAT IT TOOK ME FROM DECEMBER UNTIL May to bring out the paper. The truth is that I agreed at once. The delay was due chiefly to the fact that Peter, in his optimism about funds, was relying on a priest he knew who had a very plush rectory uptown on the West Side. His clerical friend would give us a mimeograph machine, paper, and space in the rectory basement. None of these were forthcoming—they had been only optimistic notions of Peter's.

But in the meantime Peter was educating me. I had had a secular education, he said, and he would give me a Catholic outline of history. One way to study history was to read the lives of the saints down the centuries. Perhaps he chose this method because he had noticed my library, which contained a life of St. Teresa of Avila and her writings, especially about her spiritual foundations, and a life of St. Catherine of Siena. "Ah, there was a saint who had an influence on her times!" he exclaimed. Then he plunged into a discussion of St. Catherine's letters to the Popes and other public figures of the fourteenth century, in which she took them to task for their failings.

The date I had met Peter is clear in my mind because it was just after the feast of the Immaculate Conception, which is on December 8. I had visited the national shrine at Catholic University in Washington to pray for the hunger marchers. I felt keenly that God was more on the side of the hungry, the ragged, the unemployed, than on the side of the comfortable churchgoers who gave so little heed to the misery of the needy and the groaning of the poor. I had prayed that some way would open up for me to do something, to line myself up on their side, to work for them, so that I would no longer feel that I had been false to them in embracing my new-found faith.

The appearance of Peter Maurin, I felt with deep conviction, was the result of my prayers. Just as the good God had used the farmer Habakkuk to bring the mess of food intended for the reapers to Daniel in the lions' den, so had He sent Peter Maurin to bring me the good intellectual food I needed to strengthen me to work for Him.

I learned shortly how he had happened to come to see me. He had heard of me on a visit to the *Commonweal*, our famous New York weekly edited by laymen. It had been started by Michael Wiliams, a veteran journalist, who had worked in San Francisco on the same paper with my father years before. Peter had also been told of my conversion by a redheaded Irish Communist with whom he struck up a conversation on a bench in Union Square. The Irishman told Peter that we both had similar ideas—namely, that the Catholic Church had a social teaching which could be applied to the problems of our day. So Peter set out to find me.

Now he had someone to whom he could propound his program. He must have proposed it many times before, at Social Action conferences, in visits to public figures and chancery offices around the country. But he seemed to have got nowhere. It might have been his shabbiness, it might have been his thick accent, that prevented him from getting a hearing.

Perhaps it was because of my own radical background that Peter brought me a digest of the writings of Kropotkin one day, calling my attention especially to *Fields, Factories and Workshops*. He had gone over to the Rand School of Social Science for this, and carefully copied out the pertinent passages. He also liked *Mutual Aid* and *The Conquest of Bread*.

I was familiar with Kropotkin only through his *Memoirs of a Revolutionist*, which had originally run serially in the *Atlantic Monthly*. (Oh, far-off day of American freedom, when Karl Marx could write for the morning *Tribune* in New York, and

Kropotkin could not only be published in the *Atlantic*, but be received as a guest in the homes of New England Unitarians, and in Jane Addams' Hull House in Chicago!)

Peter came day after day. He brought me books to read and the newest of his phrased writings. There was to be no end to my learning.

One day I chanced upon Peter in his friend's uptown church. I had dropped in to say a few prayers. After some minutes I looked up. There was Peter, sitting in front of the Blessed Sacrament, evidently in deep meditation. He seemed totally unconscious of the presence of anyone else in the church. He sat there in silence. Every now and then he would nod his head, and gesticulate with his hands, as though he were making one of his points to the Presence before Whom he sat so quietly. I did not want to disturb him.

Also, in my subconscious I was probably tired of his constant conversation. His line of thought, the books he had given me to read, were all new to me and all ponderous. There was so much theory. I had read about Kropotkin the man, his life and adventures. In a way, they told me much. I was not sure I wanted to know more. Peter read Kropotkin's theoretical works. It was the idea, the abstract thought, that got him and that he hoped would get me.

Sitting there thinking back over the past weeks, I had to face the fact that Peter was hard to listen to. I would tune in on some concert, some symphony, and beg him to be still. Tessa and I both loved music, but Peter seemed to have no ear for it. He would be obedient for a time. But soon he would look at my forbidding face and, seeing no yielding there, he would go over to the gentler Tessa. Pulling a chair close to hers and leaning almost on the arm, he would begin to talk. He was incorrigible. Yet we were growing to love him, to greet him warmly when he came, to press food on him, knowing that he ate only one meal a day.

His willingness to talk to any visitor who dropped in, however, was a boon to us; it released us for our various chores. I, for example, could run into the front room to my typewriter and get some work done. I recall one visitor in particular, who came quite often, a sculptor named Hugh—a tall man, heavy and quiet, with big brown eyes. He used to take out a flute and play while Peter talked to him.

"You are quite right, Peter," he would say every now and then, nodding absently. Then he would go right on piping his simple tunes. He startled us one day, when a woman friend of ours came to call, by remarking after she had left that she used to come to his studio and sit in the nude on the mantelpiece. We concluded that she must have resembled some model who had once posed for him.

Usually by ten or eleven we urged our visitors to go. We were at home with them and felt free to send them on their way. On mild nights, Hugh and Peter would go on to Union Square to sit on a park bench. There they would continue their conversation— if it could be called that—with Hugh playing his flute, and Peter, gesticulating, haranguing him with his discussion of history, his analysis of ideas, old and new, and, in doing so, perhaps rehearsing his lessons for me for the next day.

Placidly, Tessa awaited her baby, and I went on with my free-lancing. In the evenings, my brother and I (John was working days now) would talk over plans for the paper with Peter, who knew nothing at all about journalism. He would supply the ideas, and we would get out the paper for the "man in the street."

My mind and heart were full of the part I had to play, self-centered creature that I was. I planned the makeup and the type, and what stories I would write to go with Peter's easy essays. I don't think we even consulted Peter as to whether he liked the title we had given to his writings in the paper, "Easy Essays." He was so happy over the coming incarnation of his ideas in print that he never expressed himself on the subject. But he well knew that, in spite of the title, his essays were anything but easy. Like those in the Gospel, his were hard sayings—hard to work out in everyday life.

Having become convinced of this after several weeks, I went, on the advice of Father Joseph McSorley, former provincial of the Paulist Society and my good spiritual adviser at the time, to the Paulist Press. For an edition of two thousand copies, I was told, the price would be fifty-seven dollars.

I decided to wait until I had the cash in hand before getting out the first issue. I didn't want to run up any debts. I did no installment buying, although I didn't mind being late with the rent or skimping on groceries to speed the accumulation of enough money to pay the first bill. Father McSorley helped a lot by finding work for me to do. Father Harold Purcell gave me ten dollars, and Sister Peter Claver brought me a dollar which someone had just given to her.

All that winter Peter had come back and forth from Mt. Tremper in upstate New York, but by April he was in town all the time. Our plans were shaping up. Yet Peter was plainly not too well pleased with the way the paper was going.

I had sent my copy to the printer—news accounts of the exploitation of Negroes in the South, and the plight of the sharecroppers; child labor in our own neighborhood; some recent evictions; a local strike over wages and hours; pleas for better home relief, and so on—and we were waiting for proofs.

When they came we cut them out and started making a dummy, pasting them up on the eight pages of a tabloid the size of *The Nation*, writing headlines, and experimenting with different kinds of type. Peter looked over what I had written as it came back from the printer. I could see that, far from being happy about it, he was becoming more and more disturbed. One day, while looking over some fresh proofs, he shook his head. His expression was one of great sadness.

"It's everyone's paper," he said. I was pleased. I thought that was what we both wanted. "And everyone's paper is no one's paper," he added with a sigh.

He rose without another word and went out the door. Later we learned indirectly that he had gone back upstate. It was some time before we heard from him again.

We kept hoping that he would be on hand for that historic May Day in 1933 when we ventured out in Union Square to sell the first issue. He wasn't. A friendly priest sent three young men to ac-

*On May Day, 1934, Catholic Workers tried to sell
their paper to Communists in Union Square.
The sixth figure from the left is Earl Browder.*

company me. One of them was Joe Bennett, a tall, gangling blond
boy from Denver, who was to work closely with us for some
months. The day was bright and warm and beautiful. The square
was packed with demonstrators and paraders, listening to speeches,
carrying on disputes among themselves, or glancing through the
great masses of literature being given out or sold, which so soon
were litter on the ground.

The two younger men, intimidated and discouraged by the
slighting comments of the champions of labor and the left, soon

fled. Religion in Union Square! It was preposterous! If we had been representing Jehovah's Witnesses, we might have had a friendlier reception. But people associated with the Roman Catholic Church! Joe Bennett and I stuck it out, reveling in the bright spring sunshine. We did not sell many papers, but we did enjoy the discussions into which we were drawn. One Irishman looked at the masthead and rebuked us for the line which read "a penny a copy." We were in the pay of the English, he said. Next month we changed it to "a cent a copy" just to placate the Irish.

We knew Peter would not have let this go without making a point. He would have said, "When an Irishman met an Irishman a thousand years ago, they started a monastery. Now, when an Irishman meets an Irishman, you know what they start!" Then he would have gone on with a long discourse on Gaelic culture, on how it was the Irish who kept civilization alive through the Dark Ages, and on and on, until his adversary would have forgotten all about his heat over the penny.

Another protest came from a Negro, who pointed out that the two workers on our masthead, standing on either side of our title, *The Catholic Worker*, were both white men. One had a pick and the other had a shovel. "Why not have one white and the other colored?" he wanted to know.

We thought it was a good suggestion. Before our next issue came out we found an artist who made a new masthead for us, a white man and a colored man, each with his implements of toil, clasping hands, with the figure of Christ in the background, uniting them. Joe Bennett and I sat on park benches that first day, got our first touch of sunburn, and gradually relaxed. In spite of our small sales and the uncertain prospects for the future, it was with a happy feeling of accomplishment that I returned to East Fifteenth Street that evening.

But I missed Peter Maurin. We had been so excited at the idea of launching a new paper, small though it was, and we had had so many details to attend to, that there was not much time to miss him before the paper came out. But now I did. His absence gave me an uneasy feeling, reminding me that our paper was not reflecting his thought, although it was he who had given us the idea.

Then, for a while, I was too busy again to think much about it. Copies had to be mailed out to editors of diocesan papers and to men and women prominent in the Catholic world. Mail began to come in praising our first effort. Some letters even contained donations to help us continue our work. I was lightheaded with success. We had started. Tessa's baby was born the week after *The Catholic Worker* was launched. A few days later my brother got a job editing the small-town paper in Dobbs Ferry, up the Hudson River, and moved his family there.

At the same time a barbershop on the street floor below our apartment became empty. I could see that it would be ideal for an office. It was a long shop, and narrow. In back of it was a bedroom, and beyond that a kitchen. A door opened on the backyard, and the paved space in front of the garden made an ideal spot for an outdoor sitting room where we could receive guests and even serve afternoon tea. So, with a few pieces of second-hand furniture—a desk, a table, a filing case, and a couple of chairs—we made still another start.

More and more people began to come. Two constant visitors at the office of *The Catholic Worker* were a thin, shabby, and rather furtive-looking pair whom Peter had picked up in Union Square earlier in the spring before he went away. To him they represented "the worker." They would listen to him untiringly and without interrupting. They were the beginning of an audience, something to build on—not very promising, but something. After one of Peter's discussions in the square, they usually followed him to my place, where, if there was not a bit of change forthcoming, there were at least bread and sweet tea. Peter would say each time, "They have no place to sleep." He was sure that I would produce the dollar needed for two beds on the Bowery. But often there was no dollar, so they stayed for lunch instead.

All the while Peter was in the country I was visited regularly by the pair of them. They always announced themselves before I opened the door: "Dolan and Egan here again." It got so that my personal friends, knowing how exasperated I was becoming at having my time taken up, used to call out upon arriving, "Dolan and Egan here again."

Thus it was with repressed impatience that I heard one day a knock on the door of my apartment above the barbershop. I stood there, braced for the familiar greeting. When it did not come, I opened the door anyway—there stood Peter Maurin.

"Peter! Where have you been?" My relief was so great that my welcome was ardent. "Where were you on May Day? Thousands of people in Union Square and not a sign of Peter!"

"Everyone's paper is no one's paper," he repeated, shaking his head. Peter seemed rested and not so dusty as usual. His gray eyes told me that he was glad to be back. While I prepared coffee and soup and put out the bread, he went on and on, and I let him, content to wait until he was eating his soup to tell him all that had been happening. When his mouth was full he would listen.

I got no explanation from him as to why he had gone away. The closest he came to it was to say wryly, with a shrug, "Man proposes and woman disposes." But he looked at me and smiled and his eyes warmed. I could see that he was happy to be back and ready to get on with his mission. He was full of patience, ready to look at me now: not as a Catherine of Siena, already enlightened by the Holy Spirit, but as an ex-Socialist, ex-I.W.W., ex-Communist, in whom he might find some concordance, some basis on which to build. But unions and strikes and the fight for better wages and hours would remain my immediate concern. As St. Augustine said, "The bottle will still smell of the liquor it once held." I continued on this track until Peter had enlightened my mind and enlarged my heart to see further, more in accord with the liberty of Christ, on which St. Paul was always speaking.

Peter took up right where he had left off, pulling a book from his pocket to continue my schooling. It might have been an encyclical on St. Francis of Assisi; or something by Eric Gill, writer, sculptor, artist, craftsman, living at that time in a community in England; or the short book *Nazareth or Social Chaos* by Father Vincent McNabb, O.P., who had encouraged that community. It was only gradually, through many conversations, that I came to understand enough of his thinking to realize why he considered the stories in the first issue of *The Catholic Worker* inadequate.

He often spoke of what he called "a philosophy of work." "Work, not wages—work is not a commodity to be bought and sold" was one of his slogans. "Personal responsibility, not state responsibility" was another. A favorite source of his was *The Personalist Manifesto* by Emmanuel Mounier, which he would go around extemporaneously translating from the French for the benefit of any who would listen. He finally persuaded Father Virgil Michel, a Benedictine priest of St. John's Abbey, in Minnesota, to translate it. Peter got it published. "A personalist is a *go-giver*, not a *go-getter*," he used to say. "He tries to give what he has instead of trying to get what the other fellow has. He tries to be good by doing good to the other fellow. He has a social doctrine of the common good. He is alter-centered, not self-centered."

Much later, when I had a look at that first issue, I could see more clearly what bothered Peter. We had emphasized wages and hours while he was trying to talk about a philosophy of work. I had written of women in industry, children in industry, of sweatshops and strikes.

"Strikes don't strike me!" Peter kept saying, stubbornly. It must have appeared to him that we were just urging the patching-up of the industrial system instead of trying to rebuild society itself with a philosophy so old it seemed like new. Even the name of the paper did not satisfy him. He would have preferred *Catholic Radical*, since he believed that radicals should, as their name implied, get at the root of things. The second issue of the paper, the June-July number, showed that we had been talking things over. My editorial said:

Peter Maurin (whose name we misspelled in the last issue) has his program which is embodied in his contribution this month. Because his program is specific and definite, he thinks it is better to withdraw his name from the editorial board and continue his contact with the paper as a contributor.

Then came Peter's editorial:

As an editor, it will be assumed that I sponsor or advocate any reform suggested in the pages of *The Catholic Worker*. I would rather definitely sign my own work, letting it be understood what I stand for.

My program stands for three things: Round-table discussions is one and I hope to have the first one at the Manhattan Lyceum the last Sunday in June. We can have a hall holding 150 people for eight hours for ten dollars. I have paid a deposit of three. I have no more money now but I will beg the rest. I hope everyone will come to this meeting. I want Communists, radicals, priests, and laity. I want everyone to set forth his views. I want clarification of thought.

The next step in the program is houses of hospitality. In the Middle Ages it was an obligation of the bishop to provide houses of hospitality or hospices for the wayfarer. They are especially necessary now and necessary to my program, as halfway houses. I am hoping that someone will donate a house rent-free for six months so that a start may be made. A priest will be at the head of it and men gathered from our round-table discussions will be recruited to work in the houses cooperatively and eventually be sent out to farm colonies or agronomic universities. Which comes to the third step in my program. People will have to go back to the land. The machine has displaced labor. The cities are overcrowded. The land will have to take care of them.

My whole scheme is a Utopian, Christian communism. I am not afraid of the world communism. I am not saying that my program is for everyone. It is for those who choose to embrace it. I am not opposed to private property with responsibility. But those who own private property should never forget it is a trust.

This succinct listing of his aims was not even the lead editorial. Perhaps it sounded too utopian for my tastes; perhaps I was irked because women were left out in his description of a house of hospitality, where he spoke of a group of men living under a priest. In addition to Peter's editorial, there were several of his easy essays. In one, recommending the formation of houses of hospitality and farming communes, he wrote in his troubadour mood:

> We need round-table discussions
> to keep trained minds from becoming academic.

> We need round-table discussions
> to keep untrained minds from being superficial.

> We need round-table discussions
> to learn from scholars
> how things would be, if they were as they should be.

> We need round-table discussions
> to learn from scholars
> how a path can be made

from things as they are
to things as they should be.

We need houses of hospitality
to give to the rich
the opportunity to serve the poor.

We need houses of hospitality
to bring the Bishops to the people
and the people to the Bishops.

We need houses of hospitality
to bring back to institutions
the technique of institutions.

We need houses of hospitality
to bring social justice
exercised in Catholic institutions.

The unemployed need free rent.
They can have that
in an agronomic university.

The unemployed need free fuel.
They can get that
in an agronomic university.

The unemployed need free food.
They can raise that
in an agronomic university.

The unemployed need to acquire skill.
They can do that
in an agronomic university.

There were other articles on more mundane matters. One stated that readers had contributed $156.50. That, with what money I got from free-lancing, would keep us going. There was also a report on distribution: papers were being mailed out all over the country in bundles of ten or twenty; Dolan and Egan had been selling on the streets (they kept the money to pay for their "eats and tobacco"); and I too had embarked on the great adventure of going out to face up to "the man in the street."

The Catholic Worker's first home was on East 15th Street in 1932. Dorothy Day, second from right, shared second-floor apartment with her brother John and his wife Tessa; Worker office on ground floor was former barbershop.

So we continued through the summer. Since this was the depression and there were no jobs, almost immediately we found ourselves a group, a staff, which grew steadily in numbers. Joe Bennett, our first salesman, was still with us. Soon we were joined by Stanley Vishnewski, a seventeen-year-old Lithuanian boy from the Williamsburg section of Brooklyn who used to walk to New York over the bridge every day and then twenty-five blocks uptown to Fifteenth Street. He sold the paper, too, and ran errands and worked without wages despite the urging of his father, a tailor, that he ought to be looking for a job. (Stanley has remained with us ever since.) A young girl, a journalism student at Columbia and a graduate of Manhattanville, also joined us at about this time.

There were also Dan Irwin, an unemployed bookkeeper, and Frank O'Donnell, who had been working as a salesman, selling people things they didn't really want, and who had a guilty conscience about it. Then there was Big Dan. I remember how he came in the first time, groaning and shouting, and, when asked what we could do for him, he bellowed, "I'd like to soak my feet!" He had been walking the streets all day, looking for a job. His shoes were worn and shabby, and did not fit him, and since it had been raining, they were wet and shrunken besides. I brought out a washtub of hot water. He gratefully took off his socks, which were full of holes, and gingerly, one after the other, put his feet into the hot water, roaring his delight. I was thinking of the time Jesus washed the feet of His apostles and then told them, "As I have done to you, so you do also." But I couldn't bring myself to do any more than offer the tub of hot water, soap, and towels. It would have been too embarrassing.

Anyone who came in was always invited to the meal being served in the kitchen—we ate in shifts when the room would not hold us all—so Big Dan stayed that evening. Between mouthfuls he told us that he had been sleeping around the piers on the waterfront. He had been eating out of garbage cans as he did not want to stay with his sister—who was perfectly ready to keep him— because she had so many kids and he had such a big appetite.

One thing Peter used to love to say—and he said it that night to Big Dan—was "People are always looking for a job. What I say is 'Fire the bosses! Fire the bosses!' "

This slogan enchanted Big Dan. He would have liked to see the boss put in *his* place, walking the streets, looking for a job. He no doubt pictured himself sitting in a fine office, in the act of "firing the boss" while he himself was gainfully employed doing nothing. His eyes sparkled as he looked at Peter.

"The boss offers his employees stock in the company and the worker gets stuck!" Peter shouted gleefully. It was hard to imagine anyone having the stock to get stuck with in those days, but he loved the word play, laughing at his own wit, which often failed to get across. The idea of being proud to be poor, however, was something that straightened Dan's shoulders. He came back early the next morning to pick up a bundle a papers to sell in Union Square. He had a reason now to stand on a street corner in touch with the passers-by.

A *Daily Worker* salesman would shout, "Read *The Daily Worker!*" Big Dan would counter with "Read *The Catholic Worker* daily!" He had a big voice and shouting slogans gave him a chance to use it. He also had a smile people could not resist. He sold lots of papers and was the best public-relations man we could have had. Besides selling on Fourteenth Street, he also ventured uptown, where he sold in front of Macy's and in front of the midtown church of St. Francis of Assisi on Thirty-first Street. One time he saw me on my way to midday Mass and began to yell, "Read *The Catholic Worker!* Romance on every page!" On another occasion he roared, "Read *The Catholic Worker*—and here comes the editor down the street!"

An unemployed girl named Mary Sheehan who joined our group also had a taste for badinage. She made the most of her keen wit in selling papers, relishing her street-corner encounters. Once a comrade jeered at her, "I know your Cardinal! He gets drunk with his housekeeper every Saturday night."

Mary snapped back, "And doesn't that show how democratic he is!"

When there was too much of this sort of play going on, Peter would at first look a little puzzled. Then he would become withdrawn. "Too much kidding, too much joshing," he would say. When things got noisy around the office, he would wander off to Union Square to find someone else to listen to him.

That summer Peter performed with gusto his role as a troubadour of God. During dinner he talked—or rather he chanted—and his essays made a pleasant accompaniment to our meals.

One of them, "A Case for Utopia," which we printed later in our paper, is especially pertinent today:

> The world would be better off
> if people tried to become better,
> and people would become better
> if they stopped trying to become better off.
> For when everyone tries to become
> better off
> nobody is better off.
> But when everyone tries to become better
> everybody is better off.
> Everyone would be rich
> if nobody tried to become richer,
> and nobody would be poor
> if everybody tried to be the poorest.
> And everybody would be what he ought to be
> if everybody tried to be
> what he wants the other fellow to be.

Peter would go on to tell how Mirabeau said there were three ways to make a living—begging, stealing, and working. "But stealing is against the law of God and the law of man. Begging is against the law of man, but not against the law of God. Work, on the other hand, is against neither the law of God nor the law of man. But they say there is no work to do. There is *plenty* of work to do." His voice would rise, for this was a clarion call with Peter. "But there are no wages. Well, people do not need to work for wages. They can offer their services as a gift."

At first, Big Dan looked at Peter with astonishment. But noticing our own respectful attention, he ate—and, I think, listened. He heard Peter's ideas often enough to make them, however grudgingly, a part of his life. He never did quite get the idea of working without wages; his little income from selling the paper on the street meant a lot to him. He could tell his sister he was working for board and room, and he had a few coins now to jingle in his pocket.

"To work without wages!" Here was the saying that made people turn away, shrugging their shoulders. How hard this was to take! We none of us realized how much feeling of class war there was in our attitudes, how much resentment, how much readiness to assume that everyone was trying to take advantage of the worker, to get all he could out of him.

Even now I often think, "What an inspired attitude Peter took in his painful and patient indoctrination—and what a small part of it we accepted." He had the simplicity of an Alyosha, a Prince Mishkin. He accepted gratefully what people offered, finding plenty of work to do, always taking the least place—and serving others.

Chapter 3

Houses of Hospitality

"WE NEED HOUSES OF HOSPITALITY," PETER SAID, "TO GIVE TO THE rich an opportunity to serve the poor."

Our first house of hospitality came into being very shortly after *The Catholic Worker* did—while we were working on the second issue, in fact—in the barbershop we had taken below our Fifteenth Street apartment. A young woman, an unemployed textile worker about to have a baby, took charge of the kitchen and busied herself preparing meals for the homeless men who had already begun drifting in. It wasn't long before we were all eating in shifts.

The garden proved to be a fine place for coffee and talk. Young people flocked in, intent on putting their own social ideas into practice. The college students were often more disposed to discuss and argue than to work, and the old war between thinker and worker broke out at once. Peter welcomed the conflict. "It makes for clarification of thought," he said happily.

One day a professor of philosophy from the Catholic University dropped in. He discoursed all day on "War and Christian Morals." As we served him his meals in the garden, the talk went on and on, people coming and going. Another time a Russian doctor, a German Benedictine priest, and a Mexican general were there all talking at once, each espousing his particular cause in his own accent. The Russian favored theocracy; the German priest talked of "victim souls"; and the Mexican, inflamed by the persecutions then going on, wanted us to help raise arms for a counter-revolution. Peter, in the interests of clarification of thought, talked in his French accent of farming communes.

By fall, letters pouring in from all over the country indicated that *The Catholic Worker* was a success. Running through these letters, Peter became so dazzled by them that, in the interests of further clarification of thought, he decided to take a bold step: he hired the ballroom of the Manhattan Lyceum, which was usually reserved for weddings and bar mizvahs. He planned a series of Sunday afternoon lectures and discussions. He went so far as to advertise his first lecture with mimeographed leaflets. About fifteen people showed up.

After that he contented himself with a small meeting room. But the gatherings were soon taken over by two young political actionists whose ambition it was to soapbox in the slums and start a Catholic political party. Overridden and shouted down, Peter walked quietly back to his benches in Union Square and we quit paying the rent on the room. The young men thought this uncharitable of us and accused us of not permitting freedom of speech.

I tried to comfort Peter (not that he needed comforting) by telling him of Lenin's widow, Madame Krupskaya, who wrote in her autobiography of the workers' schools which she and her husband had held in the parks of Paris and in the woods. At one such gathering on a Sunday afternoon there had been forty people! It was counted a success.

We had a workers' school of our own at the office that first winter. Peter invited all kinds of notables—famous priests and teachers—and many were the arguments that developed. Every night in the week there was a new speaker with whom Peter could take issue. He was never tired, for he had already acquired the habit of staying up until two or three in the morning, or as long as a discussion lasted, and then sleeping the next morning until just in time to get up for noonday Mass. I sometimes wondered if he were trying to emulate Marx and Proudhon, who once argued all night and then continued their argument all the way across the English Channel without ever coming to any agreement.

The best was none too good for the poor, we thought, so we had such priests as Father La Farge, S.J., Father Joseph McSorley, and Father Paul Hanly Furfey of Catholic University, not to mention such distinguished visitors as Jacques Maritain and Hilaire Belloc.

By coming to us, these men were now able to reach many more than the few dozen who crowded into the old store on East Fifteenth Street. Students and others in groups similar to ours which had already sprung up around the country were able to read their writings in *The Catholic Worker*, to ponder their thought, and to try making the synthesis of "cult, culture and cultivation," which Peter was always talking about.

The talks on liturgy and worship and scripture fell under the head of "cult." But, since the meetings included those of other faiths, they were also ecumenical. They were, in fact, the beginning of our work for peace among religious groups. We could all meet together, Peter pointed out, in our search for the common good. Culture was an outgrowth of cult, and Peter gave us digests of Eric Gill's writings and invited artists and writers to speak to us. Under "cultivation" the land movement and cooperatives were discussed.

While these talks were going on, Stanley, and Margaret, our cook, and Mary Sheehan used to sit out in the kitchen. Once Stanley said in awestruck tones, "If we paid these men for their lectures they would get a hundred dollars apiece."

"If they're so great," Mary would say, reaching for the coffeepot, "why don't you sit in there and listen to them?" And Margaret would shush them both in her own high, shrill voice.

One evening an old Russian friend, André Salama, showed up with a great loaf of East Side rye bread, a pot of sweet butter, plenty of zakuska, and a bottle of vodka. While the meeting went on in the front office, we had a feast around the kitchen table. Salama had come to tell me about some wonderful prayers to the Mother of God, prayers very much like our own to the Mother of God, which he had found in the Russian liturgy. Every now and then he sang them lustily between his hearty quaffs of vodka.

Revelry and serious discussions—they went together in those early years. It was only when some of the young fellows who had come to help us showed signs of being alcoholics that the rest of us gave up these pleasures. Peter set the example. As soon as the situation became clear to him, he refused the glass of wine which we had been offering him at closing time when we put out the lights for the night and went to our various abodes.

Presently we rented an apartment down the street to house our first group of women guests—about half a dozen then—and took another place behind old St. Brigid's Church, on Seventh Street, to accommodate the men. Life was not all peaceful, by any means, for some of them drank, but the real problem that continued to dog us was space. When a priest on the West Side, on the edge of Greenwich Village, urged us to rent an old house in his parish, we moved. The new quarters, on Charles Street, were somewhat bigger; at least we could all be together in one place and in that way shore each other up. In the course of the year we were able to spend there, we started a maternity guild and a workers' school. By then, of course, we were already quite experienced in such matters as collecting and distributing clothes, while the kitchen detail continued to work overtime.

But we needed still more room. One of our readers, Gertrude Burke, who had inherited some tenements on lower Mott Street, offered us the use of an abandoned rear building if we would collect the rent on the buildings in the front. I went down to look it over. My first reaction was one of righteous indignation that anyone would be willing to ask for rent on such a place, so I refused her offer.

Then, as more and more people came to us and we were more and more hard-pressed, I thought again of Miss Burke and repented of my rashness. She often came to visit us with a friend, a retired telegrapher named Mary Lane. Mary's blind faith in our integrity was a constant reassurance to Gertrude, who had frequent qualms over our lack of conformity with the viewpoint of the diocesan press. I wondered whether I should not reopen the question with her and ask if she wouldn't let us have the rear building without any obligation to collect rents.

Around that time I had a speaking engagement at the Good Shepherd Convent in Troy, New York. This convent, like other similar ones, housed young women committed to them by the courts on all kinds of charges. Connected with the convent is a house of the Magdalenes, an order within an order, made up of women who have sinned and repented. They are strictly cloistered, and the active and more honored nuns treat them with reverence and depend on their prayers. I was given the privilege of speaking with the Magdalenes. While telling them about our women in need, I asked them especially to pray for a bigger house for us. Then, thinking of the admonition "Pray as though all depended on God, and work as though all depended on yourself," I wrote my letter to Miss Burke.

Her reply came within a week. We should have accepted her offer in the first place, she wrote, for she had willed both houses to the widows who ran the House of Calvary, a hospital for poor cancer patients in the Bronx. Nevertheless, she said she had asked them if we could have the use of the empty rear building, and they had consented.

The generosity of these women was remarkable. They waited, at first, to discover what use we would make of the twenty-room building. Then, when they saw the plastering and painting that went on, they paid for some heavy repairs which they knew we could not possibly do ourselves. Later they put up a new fire escape and improved the building by constructing "fire-retarding halls." And, not least of all, they serenely endured a lot of complaints from neighbors about our growing family. We were never sure who actually footed the repair bills; it might have been Gertrude Burke, and then again it might have been the widows. Had it been the former, the widows might well have looked wistfully (one could not say grudgingly) at the money spent on us, which could have been given to their more deserving charity. As Dwight MacDonald, who wrote a series about us for *The New Yorker*, said, our mission seemed to be the *un*deserving poor. But, given the widows' exalted outlook, they probably figured that if we saved one soul we were worth our keep. (One soul, it has been said, is enough bishopric for any bishop.)

Since The Catholic Worker is a movement rather than an accredited charitable organization, the widows even paid our taxes. The point we make of emphasizing personal responsibility, rather than state or organized responsibility, has cost us a good deal through the years, but in this instance it was costing them.

We were to live on Mott Street for fourteen years, from 1936 to 1950. As we needed more room, we rented apartments in the front building when they became empty, until finally we were occupying thirty-eight rooms and two stores.

The breadlines were not long in forming. In an old issue of the paper I find this description, written in the mid-thirties, which gives a good picture of the lines in those grim days:

ON THE COFFEE LINE

By One of the Servers

Having spent most of the night in heated discussion and neglecting the time, I was in no mood to crawl out at 5:30 this morning to do a turn on the breadline. But the quickest way to forget sleepiness is to roll out, wet my face and turn on the radio in the store—this I did.

It is hard to cut a mountain of bread and prepare it for serving. I say hard because it seems hours before the job is complete. The eyes of the men outside peering in keep saying—it's cold out here, or, he's about ready now. The bread is all set (this about 6:15) and Scotty has the first 100 gallons of steaming coffee ready to serve and we open the door.

On a cold morning such as this I can imagine the stream of hope that flows through the long line right down Mott Street and around the corner on Canal. Cups are taken and the three-hour session of feeding our friends is under way. I can watch the faces and see thanks written between the lines denoting age and fatigue and worry.

Ade Bethune's drawings always arrest the attention of the men for a moment. No matter how anxious they are about reaching the coffee pot there is always time to cast eyes along the wall. Many are old faces who come every morning. One I call the "Cardinal" because of his purple knitted cap so worn and shy of edges it looks like a skull cap. He always has a kindly word. As usual my Japanese friend comes early. He too always has a greeting.

Now today there are three youngsters with unkempt hair, wrinkled clothes and looking very tired. Knocking around the country with no place to wash or get cleaned, is new to them. In spite of their youth and strength the condition is more obvious. The oldsters are more used to it. Every morning there are several who carry shopping bags or bundles with their last few belongings. They place them under the table so as to better handle a hot cup and a huge chunk of bread.

One of the regular bundle-toters had a new coat this morning. All winter he has had a trench coat heavy with the dirt of many night's sleeping out and smoke from many a fire. His new coat must have belonged to some stylish young boy with extreme taste. In spite of this he looked better, the coat was warmer and he had a more confident air.

I am relieved now to go to Mass which means I must pass a whole block of hungry, waiting men. It seems a long walk some mornings, especially when it is cold or wet. I receive greetings from those who have come to know us. I wish many more would pass them during their long days to give them a chance to share and realize their troubles. The line is broken at the corner so as to enable pedestrians to pass. The line running west on Canal Street extends for about 200 feet. It is really impossible then, to forget them at Mass.

On returning it is easy to recognize the familiar hats, coats, shoes, and other misfitting clothing of the regular comers. All, after being out for hours in the cold, are hunched against the weather and have their hands in their pockets. Across the street three are at a fire made of cardboard boxes. The huge flames will soon die away. There is one Negro and two aged white men. None talk but just stare at the flames, absorbing the heat and probably seeing better days gone by.

I can recognize one of my regular friends. He is a midwesterner with an attractive drawl. He lives his nights in subway trains. The newspapers in his pockets he has picked up from trains and generally gives them to us. A small gift indeed but a gift given out of real appreciation. He is tanned because of two warm days sitting in the park facing the new spring sun and catching up on much needed sleep.

Here comes the little Irishman who will ask for the softest kind of bread. He has no teeth and cannot chew the crusts of the rye bread. He appreciates our remembering this and he knows we will have some kind of soft bread ready.

They continue to come. When I am busy putting peanut butter on bread and can't see their faces I can recognize the arms that reach for bread. One gets to know all the familiar marks of the garments. The hands of some tremble from age, sickness or drink. It is near closing time and the line thins out. They must go out now into a world seemingly full of people whose hearts are as hard and cold as the pavements they must walk all day in quest of their needs. Walk they must for if they sit in the park (when it is warm) the police will shoo them off. Then there is the worry of the next meal or that night's sleeping arrangements. Here starts their long weary trek as to Calvary. They meet no Veronica on their way to relieve their tiredness nor is there a Simon of Cyrene to relieve the burden of the cross. It is awful to think this will start again tomorrow.

It sometimes seemed that the more space we had, the more people came to us for help, so that our quarters were never quite adequate. But somehow we managed. Characters of every description and from every corner of life turned up—and we welcomed them all. They "joined" The Catholic Worker in many ways. Some came with their suitcases, intending to stay with us a year, and, shocked by our poverty, lingered only for the night. Others came for a weekend and remained for years. Someone visiting us simply to challenge some "point" made in an article in the paper would become a permanent member of our community. A seventy-year-old man named Mr. Breen strode in one day with a cane and a fountain pen, sat down at a table without a word, and, in a beautiful calligraphy, began to answer a trayful of letters. His task completed, he announced he was staying for good.

Mr. Breen is someone we will not soon forget. A former newspaperman, his talk was filled with words like "kikes," "dinges" and "dagos," and he prided himself on his family background, education, and penmanship. His wife and children had all died, and at the age of seventy he found himself destitute, living in the municipal lodging house. There were thousands being sheltered there that winter; Mr. Breen's greatest affliction was having to share the hospitality of the city with Negroes. He had been put off home relief because he was always threatening the investigators with his cane. He was beaten up one night at the lodging house (age is no protection there) for his racist attitudes. Wandering around the next morning, he discovered us.

Mr. Breen's racism was not long in showing itself. It caused us difficulties, but it did give us a chance to practice our pacifism. At about the time of his arrival, a Negro had come to us. He was good-looking and ambitious, with a deep, resonant voice. He loved to read aloud. His great hope was to become a radio announcer. He had no interest whatever in racial justice; he thought

This Catholic Worker breadline was typical of many in the 1930's. Worker headquarters on Mott Street was near heart of Chinatown.

only in terms of getting ahead. He felt himself above a̲i̲
labor, choosing instead to type or file or perform so̲r̲ᵃl
kind of clerical work, all of which he did badly. Cons̲ᵉr
we were of the indignities his people had suffered at theˢ
of our own white race, our collective guilt made us put up
him in spite of his behavior, which was, at times, insufferable.

From their first encounter, Mr. Breen took delight in insult.
him. Mr. Rose, the Negro, promptly found ways to get even. In
my absence, he would sit at my desk, put his feet up on it, and
taunt Mr. Breen with the liking white women had for colored
men. Upon my return, Mr. Breen would vent his spleen on me,
calling me a "nigger lover."

Whenever we heard Mr. Breen roaring while we were doing
the household chores, we would rush in to find out what was the
matter. We would see Mr. Rose sitting calmly at his desk, ap-
pearing to be working diligently, while Mr. Breen, his dirty
white hair tossing, his eyes bulging out of his apoplectic face,
stood over him, sputtering with rage. (Mr. Breen did, indeed,
have several strokes that winter, once narrowly escaping death.)

He lived in a little hall bedroom; he had the old newspaperman's habit of reading all the papers, then dropping them around
him when he had finished. Aware of the danger, we picked up
after him as best we could, but we couldn't keep him from
getting at matches and cigarettes. One night, after lighting a
cigarette, he was unable to shake out the flame of his match. He
just dropped it, still burning, among the papers and set fire to
them. Fortunately, another guest was nearby at the time, a guest
about whom we knew nothing except that his name was Mr.
Freeman and that he said he had been a rabbi and become a
Catholic. He tried to rescue Mr. Breen, but all the while the old
man kept beating him off with his cane and calling him a "god-
damn Jew." But Mr. Freeman saved him anyway.

Mr. Breen remained with us until he died. As the end drew
near, we all sat around his bedside, taking turns saying the rosary.
In his last moments, Mr. Breen looked up at us and said,

"I have only one possession left in the world—my cane. I want

have it. Take it—take it and wrap it around the necks of
of these bastards around here."

hen he turned on us a beatific smile. In his weak voice he
spered,

"God has been good to me."

And smiling, he died.

"A house of hostility," Stanley used to say, after incidents like
this. Sometimes we did feel sad, indeed, when our houses seemed
to be filled more with hate and angry words than with the love
we were seeking.

But as St. John of the Cross said, "Where there is no love, put
love and you will take out love."

Despite Peter's oft-repeated dictum, "Strikes don't strike me,"
we did what we could by word and deed to help the worker in
his fight for better conditions and higher wages. Every issue of
the paper was crowded with labor news; the thirties was a time
of great struggle for workers, of course, and at one point we
printed a large box headed "July 4th News—Independence Day"
with twenty-three separate sections, each summarizing the present
state of a major strike then going on somewhere around the
nation.

One of the first strikes we participated in directly was a
brewery workers' strike. (We pointed out that their work was
a work of mercy because they gave drink to the thirsty!) Writing
about the strike, I stressed the idea of cooperative ownership and
management referred to in Pius XI's encyclical "Forty Years
After," to raise the worker from the proletariat. (John XXIII,
in "Mater et Magistra," was to continue along the same lines
much later.)

A year and a half later the famous seamen's strike broke out in
New York, and we not only gave cheer and *The Catholic Worker*
to the men on the picket lines but went so far as to open a
special strike branch on the West Side, which became a hangout
for many of the idle seamen. We fed thousands of them a day
there. Huge coffee pots were on the stove, and we had kegs of
peanut butter and cottage cheese and jam, and bread without

limit. At first we paid for everything. After our money gave out, we ran up bills for everything, and were left with a debt of three thousand dollars by the time the strike had run its three-month course. People are always glad to donate money to "charity," but when it is a question of hungry strikers many call them "Communists" and refuse to help. Nevertheless, we begged St. Joseph himself, and he, as always, came to our aid. I cannot improve on a worker's account of an incident that occurred early that January, 1937:

Use Terrorism Upon Seamen . . . Rock Thrown Thru Window of Catholic Worker's Strike Branch

. . . At 3 a.m. last Tuesday a New Year's present was delivered to the Catholic Worker (Waterfront Branch) via the front window. It came in the form of a paving stone. We now have a new window and half of the stone is used to bolster up our stove and the other half is used to keep the bread knife sharp, as we are slicing up 150 long loaves of bread daily.

We had been writing about our house of hospitality experiment in *The Catholic Worker*, and very quickly other houses began springing up all over the country—in San Francisco, Los Angeles, Sacramento, Chicago, Detroit, Cleveland, Boston, Memphis, Pittsburgh, and a score of other cities, including London and Wigan, England. At one time there were some forty of them. All these Catholic houses were operated independently.

In one city, a second, rival house was opened by those calling themselves the "spirituals," as opposed to "the Brother Eliases" in the first house. The well-meaning "spirituals" stayed up all night drinking with their charges in order to show a delightful sense of equality with them, but in a few months they had so exhausted themselves in these good works that they had to close the house. (Another story has it that the spiritual leaders were forced to give up their attempt to run a house when it was discovered that their happy charges had taken to robbing the poor boxes of the neighboring church.)

In general, however, the houses were so truly successful that in many cases the bishops wanted more of them. They did a unique job—taking up the slack, you might say, for all the odds

Chapter 4

Communitarian Farms

BY THE MID-THIRTIES PETER MAURIN HAD ALREADY SEEN TWO OF HIS ideas become realities. *The Catholic Worker* was a going concern. The paper came out every month and our circulation was leaping with each issue, soon exceeding a hundred thousand. Houses of hospitality, stimulated by what we wrote about our own in New York, were springing up around the country. But as yet we had done nothing about another of his ideas—the farming commune and agronomic university. In this Peter saw the solution to all the ills of the world: unemployment, delinquency, destitute old age, man's rootlessness, lack of room for growing families, and hunger.

The idea captivated the young men around The Catholic Worker that winter of 1935. I do not believe the women were so sold on it. I know I was something less than enthusiastic. My daughter was then about eight, and I preferred my own home. I loved the life of the city. Especially I loved the life of the Lower East Side, where, in my neighborhood, every Italian back yard had its own fig tree and grape arbor.

When Peter talked of grass growing through the cobbles on the city streets, it brought to my mind the delight I have always felt when I see stubborn plants pushing their way toward the sun in vacant city lots. When we were children in Bath Beach, Brooklyn—we lived in many cities because my father was a roving newspaperman—we used to imitate the Italian housewives and go out in the spring to gather the first wild dandelions. I have

42

never ceased to look with longing eye on wild greens in the city. Even now, when I walk down Grand Street to Mass, I look for the weed called "lamb's quarters," which grows so abundantly in the still empty lots next to the huge cooperative apartments, and think of the bowls of cooked greens I would have concocted from them during the depression.

My love for the city has never waned. "Heaven is portrayed as a heavenly Jerusalem," I would say wistfully to Peter.

Nevertheless, in that spring of 1935 we acquired our first "farming commune" on Staten Island. Only a ferry ride across the harbor from downtown Manhattan, Staten Island abounds in open spaces and farming land, although it lies technically within the New York City limits. Our commune was in no sense what Peter had envisioned. In fact, the place was so small that we contented ourselves with calling it a "garden commune." But we did look on it as a valid training ground for the larger farm to come. I am sure Peter felt that we were too avid to get work under way, and too inclined to jump into things without proper study or planning. But we were young and felt Peter was old (he was sixty at the time). He accepted our impulsiveness with patience, just as he did our later failures on the land. He felt that everything we undertook, large or small, illustrated some "point" he wanted to make.

The garden commune had about an acre of land. The house was large, with eight bedrooms. On the first floor, in addition to the kitchen, three rooms were built in an L. They were used as meeting rooms. A wide porch ran all around the house, which perched on a little knoll overlooking Raritan Bay. To the rear was a mile-long stretch of land, which is now Wolfe Pond Park; and at the side, thick woods. Actually, the one acre was all we were equipped to cultivate. We could raise on it the vegetables we needed to feed ourselves, plus a good deal for the house in New York. Immediately, a handful from the New York house moved out to the commune. They had all sorts of backgrounds and each came for his own reasons.

With workers and scholars living so close together, the old conflict between them reappeared almost at once. The workers wanted only to work with their hands and to produce visible results. The scholars wanted these things too; but they also had a sense of their own vocation. As far as the workers could see, what the scholars mainly wanted was the opportunity for weekends in the country devoted to nonstop talking. The workers could never understand that preparing for these weekends called for very strenuous effort of a nonphysical kind: organizing discussion groups, inviting guest speakers, planning interesting programs, and so on. As a matter of fact it was the donations from visitors who wanted to express their gratitude for having enjoyed those weekend meetings that did the most to keep the manual work going. But the workers never gave the scholars any credit for this and felt at the same time that they never received enough recognition themselves.

Our philosophy was to recognize the dignity of the worker. But too often this only seemed to swamp the humility which would have led him to take direction, and to build up his pride. Because the scholar was reluctant to exert authority, the worker, instead of thinking of the common good, was inclined to follow his own will.

But the scholar was not free of responsibility either. Too often, although motivated by the desire to avoid passing judgment on others, he would withdraw into silence. Sometimes it was the scholar's inability to communicate except to his peers that prevented the workers from following him. It was only natural for them to want a genial companion, rather than a silent, aloof, or a glibly articulate one.

Peter liked to get the students out in the garden and there, between the rows of beans, hoe in hand, he would start teaching.

"Bishop von Ketteler says that we are bound under pain of mortal sin to relieve the extreme needs of our poorer brother with our superfluous goods. But with our superfluous goods we build white elephants like the Empire State Building. With our superfluous goods we build power houses which increase producing power and therefore increase unemployment. With our superfluous goods we build colleges which turn students out into a changing world without telling them how to keep it from changing or how to change it to suit college graduates."

Each one of those statements was good for a day of discussion: about charity, personal responsibility, and state responsibility; about the machine age, and unemployment; handicrafts and village industries and decentralization; about what kind of a world college graduates really wanted.

Peter's audience would begin to dwindle as the scholars, their muscles tired from the unaccustomed work, wandered away from the bean rows. So, book in hand, he would reinforce his ideas by getting us to plunge seriously into reading. His recommended reading opened up a new world. It was he who introduced us to Don Luigi Sturzo and his ideas of the corporative order as opposed to the corporate state, as well as to Kropotkin.

Such reading has led us to a study of the *kibbutzim* of Israel and the different kinds of cooperative, collective, communal, and state farms, voluntarily undertaken with the help of generous Jews throughout the world. Eric Fromm, Martin Buber with his *Paths in Utopia*, Vinoba Bhave and Jayaprakash Narayan in India, and Danilo Dolci in Sicily—these are the men who are now pointing to the new synthesis which Peter was seeking.

"First of all," Peter used to say, "one must give up one's life to save it. Voluntary poverty is essential. To live poor, to start poor, to make beginnings even with meager means at hand, this is to get the 'green revolution' under way.

"St. Francis of Assisi thought that to choose to be poor is just as good as marrying the most beautiful girl in the world. Most of us seem to think that Lady Poverty is an ugly girl and not the beautiful girl St. Francis says she is. And because we think so, we refuse to feed the poor with our superfluous goods. Instead, we let the politicians feed the poor by going around like pickpockets, robbing Peter to pay Paul."

The young intellectuals on the farm, the college students, could not understand why we "threw our money away" on the "unworthy destitute"—for so they characterized the men on our breadlines—who had grown to alarming numbers in town. We would do better, they thought, to put money into a farming commune as a pilot project which would point the way to thousands of others all over the country. They overlooked the fact that the kinds of people who were attracted to our garden commune—themselves included—were, without doubt, the last people in the world capable of making a foundation, setting an example, or leading a way.

There was, for instance, a former drug addict who had conquered his habit but sunk to destitution. He knew several languages and Peter tried to persuade him to hold classes in French and Spanish. But no, he preferred to spend his time inventing a new language, a universal one—something like Esperanto, which he also knew. This man moved in with us on the garden commune and stayed a year. His great delight was to walk on the beach; he tried to be helpful and save coal by picking up damp driftwood and old shoes and shoving them into the furnace all winter. This often put out the fire and made more work for those who ran the house. On one occasion, he stuffed the furnace with asbestos, thinking it was just heavy paper.

There was a young boy dying of heart trouble who had to be given bed care; there was a teacher who had come to us to recover from a love affair, and still had her mind on it. There was a whole group who used to go along the beach and collect clay from the banks. They enjoyed themselves (the idea was that they were practicing crafts) making dishes and bowls. This might have been viewed as a harmless and tranquilizing occupation except that they were always washing the clay, their utensils, and their hands in the kitchen sink, frequently stopping up the plumbing.

Peter would have been quite content with the acre on Staten Island. But the young people wanted land, acreage, and animals. So the planning for a farming commune continued through the winter of that year, 1935. I remember trying to listen one Saturday afternoon to a broadcast of *Aïda* while the young people talked about the land. We were having a bitterly cold winter; outside, sooty snow lay heavy on the ground; an icy film covered the sidewalks, and the sky was leaden. Inside, we shivered. The pipes were always freezing, and even when they weren't the house was hard to heat. We tried to forget our discomfort by looking forward to next summer.

Each pictured the commune in terms of his own desires. Eddie was a printer; he spoke of setting up a little press on the farm to bring in a cash income. Bill was in love; he dreamed of building a house. Jim was a machinist; he saw himself sitting behind a tractor, pulling a plow or driving a truck which would bring vegetables to town for the soup line.

In the midst of all this talk, action was precipitated by a letter from one of our readers, a teacher in a Southern town. She also seemed enchanted by the idea of a farming commune where she could spend her summer vacations, living a liturgical life on the land. She offered to contribute a thousand dollars toward a farm on condition that we would build her a little house for which she would provide the materials. She would take three acres with it. This, she pointed out, would give work to the unemployed— but it would not be "pauperizing people and contributing to their delinquency," as she felt we were doing by maintaining our breadlines.

We were somewhat less than enthusiastic about the character of our future comrade on the land as it was suggested by her letter. We were not sure we would like anyone who wrote as she did about our beloved poor. I tried to discourage her by describing, in detail, the kind of people we were, the kind of people she would have to live with. I explained that we were not a community of saints but a rather slipshod group of individuals who were trying to work out certain principles—the chief of which was an analysis of man's freedom and what it implied. We could not put people out on the street, I said, because they acted irrationally and hatefully. We were trying to overcome hatred with love, to understand the forces that made men what they are, to learn something of their backgrounds, their education, to change them, if possible, from lions into lambs. It was a practice in loving, a learning to love, a paying of the cost of love.

Our teacher friend replied, still insisting that we start to look for a farm. So we borrowed a car and started our search all over the icy roads of New Jersey. On April 19, the feast of St. Isadore the Farmer, we found a promising property high on a hilltop, three miles out of Easton, Pennsylvania. I will never forget that lovely spring day. Big Dan, who was our driver, flung himself down on the grass and shouted ecstatically, "Back to the land!"

Mrs. Dubrow, the farmer's wife, gave us supper of mashed potatoes, stewed dried mushrooms, asparagus and home-preserved berries. It thrilled us to think that everything we were eating had been raised on that soil. The farm seemed to be just what we wanted. There were a beautiful woodlot and one or two level fields. The rest of the ground was all hilly. It was a climb up to the barn, a race down to the spring, and a climb back up to the pasture.

We could buy it for twelve hundred and fifty dollars from the Polish family then working it. This was within our reach. We could get the thousand from our teacher friend, and could easily beg the extra two hundred and fifty. We were so content with the look of the place that we made a down payment then and there, and returned to New York with fresh eggs, dandelion greens, and a great sense of a move forward. "You do not know," St. Francis said, "what you have not practiced." How could we write about farming communes unless we had one?

Only later did we find out that there was no water on all of our twenty-eight acres—only storage cisterns to catch the rain water from the barn and house. The spring to which we had run with such joy turned out to be on an adjoining farm. A few weeks later the seamen's strike broke out in New York. When a group approached us for aid, we became so occupied with providing hospitality for twenty of them that we had to delegate the job of opening up the farm to Jim and a Midwestern college student. The two of them closed the house on Staten Island and moved our belongings—mostly things which had been donated by friends and readers of *The Catholic Worker*—to the new place, which we called Maryfarm. That first summer, the house, barn, and carriage shed were all crowded.

Mr. Johnson, an invalid and a former editor whom we got to know during the National Biscuit strike, and his wife went down to take charge of the house. They also looked after my young daughter. The attic was promptly made into a dormitory for men. Among our first guests were some of the striking seamen. The two extra bedrooms were occupied by women.

Gertrude Burke, who had procured for us use of the old Mott Street tenement house, helped greatly by sending us half a dozen children at a time from Harlem and generously paying for their board. We put them up in the barn, where the college girls, who began to arrive in June, could look after them.

Actually, hers was the only such forethought. All too often, priests and sisters and other readers of the paper would send us alcoholics or mental cases just out of a hospital. But it never occurred to them to send money for their food. We were expected to raise that. And, after all, this was perfectly natural. Hadn't we written that we could live off the land? Now it was up to us to prove that we could do it. The dear Lord, however, always evened things up. Other priests and nuns sent us gifts. If we accepted in Christ the poor ones who were brought to us, then the Heavenly Father recognized that we had need of many things. We blundered our way into farming, making many mistakes. One college graduate rooted up half the valuable asparagus bed to put in vegetables of his own choosing; another rooted up all the sweet potatoes, thinking they were some kind of wild vine.

We were lucky—or guided—in other respects, as in the way we got our cow. Two of our Kansas readers, a couple named Rosenberg, sent us money for a cow (which we afterward named "Rosie" in their honor). But we hadn't the least idea what to look for in a cow.

Eddie the printer had done some milking on vacations in his childhood. One day he set out with Jim the mechanic and Cy, a college student, for a neighboring farm to negotiate the purchase. They explained to the farmer that they could pay only $50. He showed them a field full of Holsteins and said they could take their pick. They went into the field in trepidation and came on one cow who was so gentle that she permitted them to lead her. Finding her easy to milk, they bought her on the spot and led her home over the hills. It turned out they had bought an old cow, but one who was generous with her milk. Rosie had only one drawback: as summer wore on she grew lonely for her fellows and was always pulling up her stake and running away. What with the lack of fencing, bringing her back required a good deal of yanking and hauling on the part of the three purchasers, who generally looked after Rosie together.

As farmers, perhaps, we were ridiculous, but Maryfarm was a happy home that summer and for many summers after. What a varied assortment of people had come to us! There was one man who had worked as a strong man with the circus, doing an act in which a troupe of Russian acrobats made a human pyramid on his shoulders. When the moon was full, he used to do cartwheels down the side of the hill in back of the house. He so frightened John Griffin—John, a convalescent from pneumonia, had just come to us off the Bowery and slept out in the wagon shed—that he always kept a meat axe under his pillow, or at least so he insisted.

A young seminarian who spent the summer with us brought with him a half-dozen young pigs. (They were fun, except for

John Filliger and Arthur Sheehan, recently arrived from New York, wrestle with Rosie's calf in the early days at Maryfarm, Easton, Pa.

their habit of escaping from their pen just as we were saying the rosary by the little shrine we had set up in a flower garden next to the house.)

In spite of our mistakes, a lot of things got done. John Griffin, as he recovered, built us fences and rustic benches all over the place. John the seaman, one of those who came to us during the strike, has been with us so long that he is now known as John the farmer. Frank, just out of Sing Sing, planted irises and rose-bushes, pansies, zinnias and petunias.

The war between the workers and the scholars did not get started here for quite a while. The workers could not complain that the scholars were sitting around on the rustic benches because the benches were always occupied by girls telling stories to the children or preparing vegetables. Food was short at times, but discussion was long. In the summers, especially, we were crowded with both students and teachers who came to the farm to listen to Peter Maurin's ideas. This was peacetime; and although the Popes talked of the fallacy of the armed state in which we were living, our thoughts were not on the prospect of war as the great problem of the day. Such matters as unemployment and survival of the family were uppermost in our minds.

The impressions expressed later by those who came to Mary-farm are as illuminating as they are contradictory. At one time we were visited by students from ten colleges scattered around the country. Their predominant recollection, they noted, was that they had lived on lettuce. A teacher, now working for the State Department, wrote in a long and learned article for a sociological review that he had found the farm a failure for families, but a success as a refuge for celibate seamen. (We had only three seamen there during his stay!)

A seaman described life at the farm this way:

"When I first came, I thought I was in heaven, being with all these priests and professors and college students and nice girls. I'd been drunk in every port, but I'd never been anywhere ashore, except along the waterfront. Every seaman dreams of a little piece of land he can call his own—a chicken farm he can retire to. But in the country he's afraid of being alone. He's used to the companionship of the men around him on the ship when he's at sea. So a farming commune is the answer for him. Yes," he finished, with a sigh, "I thought I was in heaven. But I soon found out that people everywhere are all pretty much alike."

Before long Jim Montague got married. He and his wife had one baby and then another. By the time there were three of them we were able to compare our own progress with the growth of a family, and we began to get it through our heads that our ideals would only be achieved slowly—oven more slowly than the development of a child. We had wanted to see them burst forth full-fledged, on their feet, as did the young calves and goats we delighted in watching.

One by one we solved our immediate problems. The first was the water problem. An unemployed taxi driver came out to the farm one day that first summer to stay with us for a while. He had convinced himself that he had a special knack for finding water and he spent his very first day digging furiously. Jim did not discover this until nightfall and then had to inform the man that he had been digging on the adjoining farm. Undismayed, the fellow went at it again the next day on our own land. This time he proved his instinct right: he found water. The following year we bought the farm next door, which had a lovely spring on it, so we had an endless supply. Our food situation improved. We had pigs and chickens and our cow. We were raising a good deal of produce in our garden. People came and went, but about twenty-five on an average lived at Maryfarm. When we had our retreats the number of our guests grew, and all of them had to be fed. Peter was happy; he was seeing one of his most cherished ideas put into practice.

Within a few years, as a result of our writings about Maryfarm and Peter Maurin Farm, other communitarian farms sprouted in many places. I cannot remember them all, but among the outstanding ones were farms at Aitkin, Minnesota; South Lyon, Michigan; Avon, Ohio; Upton, Mass.; Cuttingsville, Vermont; Oxford, Pa.; and Newburgh, New York.

There was never a time when we did not have living with us what Dostoevski calls a "friend of the family," one who moves in meekly and temporarily as a guest, and who remains permanently, to become an implacable tyrant in the household. One such friend of our family was old Maurice O'Connell, who lived to be eighty-four and who stayed with us for ten years at Maryfarm.

A few weeks before his death, when the priest came from St. Bernard's Church to anoint him, Maurice announced jauntily that he would drop in to see him next time he was in town. But his appearance there was not so casual. The occasion was a Requiem Mass, after which the body of Mr. O'Connell was laid in a grave in the cemetery behind St. Joseph's Church, up on a hillside above a river. It was a clear, springlike day, but the ground was hard underfoot. We who had known him those last ten years knelt on the cold earth around the freshly dug grave.

I thought about Mr. O'Connell as the coffin was being lowered into the ground. It was a cheap gray one. I thought then that, while Mr. O'Connell had made a coffin for me back in 1940 or so, he had never made one for himself. I felt that I should have given him mine and let Hans Tunneson, our carpenter, make me another. In the coffin he had made for me I store blankets and other bedding. He finished it with the same bright-yellow varnish that he used on the altar, the sacristy closet, and the benches he made for our chapel. The altar vestment closet and benches he made for us are still in use at Peter Maurin Farm on Staten Island, and will be for many a year to come.

Mr. O'Connell had built a comfortable little house for himself out of an old tool shed. He lived in it for all but the last year of his life, when he boarded with one of the families.

There was nothing beautiful or imaginative about Mr. O'Connell's building. It was utilitarian. He would never use secondhand materials, but demanded new pine boards and nails by the barrel. Tarpaper covered roof and sides: that was as far as any of the buildings got, not only for lack of materials but for lack of ability and initiative. There was more than one kind of poverty at Maryfarm, Easton.

He also built a little cabin for my daughter, Tamar. She had saved her Christmas and birthday money for years and had eighty-five dollars of her own. This bought enough boards at that time to put up a tiny place with double-decker beds, shelves, table and chair, and the coffin chest in which to store things. I had wanted the cabin larger so that it could be heated. It turned out to be so small that the tiniest potbelly stove made it unbearably hot. But Mr. O'Connell was adamant. "I'm making this small enough so no one but you and Tamar can sleep there." As it was, others did sleep there—transients, and sometimes the men of the farm. Later a porch was put up, L-shaped, and that was large enough to be used as a sleeping porch for six.

We had to remind ourselves very often how much Mr. O'Connell had done for us in the years we lived at Easton. Of course, other people worked with him at first: John Filliger, for one; Jim Montague worked on the Buley house; Gerry Griffin and Austin Hughes helped put up Jim's house. The truth was, though, no one could work with Mr. O'Connell long, because of his irascible disposition.

How to understand people, portray people—that is the problem. St. Paul said, "Are we comforted? It is so that you may be comforted." And so I, too, write of things as they really were, for the comfort of others—for many in this world have old or sick or sinful people with whom they have to live, whom they have to love.

Often one is accused of not telling the truth because one can tell only part of the truth. Often I write about the past because I cannot write the truth about the present. But what has occurred in the past holds good for the present. The principles remain, truth remains the same. But how to write honestly, without failing in charity?

Mr. O'Connell, like many old men, was a terror. He had come from Ireland so many years ago that he claimed he could remember when Canal Street was not a street but a canal. He was one of twenty-one children. His father was both a carpenter and an athlete. Maurice pictured him as a jaunty fellow, excelling in feats of strength, looked upon with admiring indulgence by his wife.

She, according to Maurice, nursed all her children herself, baked all her bread, spun and wove, did her housekeeping, and never failed in anything. It was, indeed, a picture of the valiant woman that Maurice used to draw for us when any of our women friends were not able to nurse their children or whenever they failed in other ways.

He was an old soldier, was Maurice, and had worn many a uniform: in South Africa, in India, and in this country. Why did he stay with us? Who can say? He had no truck with pacifists or Jews or Negroes. And as for community!

According to St. Benedict, there should be a benevolent old man at every gate to receive the visitors, to exemplify hospitality by welcoming them as other Christs.

His little cabin was by the entrance to the farm, and he never missed a visitor. But what greetings! If the visitor was shabby, he shouted at him; if well dressed, he was more suave. He had many tales to tell people who came to visit his fellows in the community. He was scarcely a subtle man. "Thieves, drunkards and loafers, the lot of them!"—thus he characterized those who made up what was intended to be a farming commune. And if anyone living on the farm exhibited any skill, Maurice would sneer at him, "What jail did ye learn that in?" One man who, after living with us for a year, became a Catholic was greeted with taunts and jeers each time he passed the cabin door. "Turncoat!" Maurice would shout, "ye'd change yer faith for a bowl of soup!"

He was ready with his fists, too; only his age protected him. Once, infuriated by a woman guest who was trying to argue him into a more cooperative frame of mind, he beat his fist against a tree and broke his knuckles. Yes, a violent and enraged man—if anyone differed with him—was Mr. O'Connell.

The first winter we began our retreat house, the barn roof was repaired by three of the men on the farm with secondhand lumber. But they had to do the job with whatever tools they could round up among themselves, for by this time, the ninth year of Mr. O'Connell's stay with us, he had all the tools locked up in his cabin, where he stood guard over them with a shotgun.

That winter, when Peter Maurin and Father Roy and the other

men had a dormitory in the barn, Mr. O'Connell became ill and was persuaded to come and be nursed there. He was kept warm and comfortable, meals were brought to him on a tray, and he soon recovered his vigor. He decided to stay for the cold months and ensconced himself by the side of the huge potbellied stove. One end of the barn was the sanctuary, separated by curtains from the center, where the stove, benches, chairs, and bookshelves were. Peter and Mr. O'Connell would sit for hours in silence, the latter with his pipe and a book, Peter motionless, his chin sunk in a heavy sweater that all but engulfed him.

Mr. O'Connell was a great reader of history, but it was hard to understand him when he was trying to make a dissertation, especially when his teeth (he refused to call them dentures) were out, as they usually were. It was a difficult few months, especially in the morning when we sang a Gregorian Mass every day. Since it took place at 7 A.M., Mr. O'Connell did not enjoy this. He had been used to sleeping until 10 or 11.

During Lent that year we were reading Newman's sermons at meals. Whether Maurice did not like Newman as an Englishman or as a convert, or whether he thought the reading was directed at him, we never knew. But, in any event, he used to stomp angrily away from the table. Stanley, who read to us, had always gotten along well with him (he had never had to work with him), but Stanley had a habit of saying, while he was reading, "This is meant for Hans," "This is meant for Dorothy." Mr. O'Connell decided the reading was meant for *him* and would put up with it no longer. He moved back to his cabin, where his meals were brought to him on a tray. When spring came, however, he did walk up to the kitchen and fetch them himself.

It was then, during spring and summer, when many retreatants came to us, that Mr. O'Connell began taking them aside to tell them that we never gave him anything to eat or anything to wear. The fact was we respected his distaste for complicated dishes. He had a standing order at the grocer's for eggs, cheese, milk, bread, margarine, and canned soups, not to speak of the supplies on our kitchen shelves, from which Maurice (or anyone else) felt free to help himself.

Our friends arriving for retreats came with generous hearts, anxious to give to the poor, to feed the hungry, and to clothe the naked. Maurice had many alms given him, and many were the packages of clothes that were addressed to him. It is wonderful that people had so charitable a spirit, I often thought, but what must they think of us, whom he accused so constantly of neglecting him? Surely they were not thinking the best of us! I find little items like these jotted down in my notebook at that time: "What to do about M's having six pairs of shoes, a dozen suits of underwear, when others go without? Peter, for instance. Is it right to let Maurice get away with taking all the tools and probably selling them for drink? Where does the folly of the Cross begin or end? I know that love is a matter of the will, but what about common sense? Father Roy is all for non-sense."

Father Roy was right, of course. "A community of Christians is known by the love they have for one another. See how they love one another!"

"Nobody can say that about us," I would groan.

"If you wish to grow in love, in supernatural love, then all natural love must be pruned as the vine is pruned. It may not look as though love were there, but have faith," Father Roy used to reply.

We were being pruned, all right. Not only through Mr. O'Connell, but on all sides. Putting it on the most natural plane, I used to think how sure our "ambassadors" (those we help) are that we believe in what we say, that all men are brothers, that we are a family, that we believe in love, not in a use of force; that we would never put them out no matter how badly we are tried. If they act "naturally," with no servility, even to an extreme of showing bitterness and hatred, then one can only count that as a great victory. We believe in a *voluntary* cooperation. Our faith in these ideas must be tried as though by fire.

And then I would look upon Maurice with gratitude and with pity, that God should have chosen him to teach us such lessons. It was as though he were a scapegoat, bearing the sins of ingratitude, hatred, venom, and suspicion directed at the rest of us, all of it gathered together in one hardy old man.

On the other hand, to continue examining these subtleties: What about this business of letting the other fellow get away with things? Isn't there something awfully smug about such piety —building up your own sanctimoniousness at the expense of the *increased* guilt of someone else? This turning the other cheek, this inviting someone else to be a potential thief or murderer, in order that we may grow in grace—how obnoxious. In that case, I believe I'd rather be the striker than the meek one struck. One would almost rather be a sinner than a saint at the expense of the sinner. No, somehow we must be saved together.

It was Father Louis Farina who finally answered that question for me. And Father Yves de Montcheuil, who died a martyr at the hands of the Gestapo because he believed principles were worth dying for. Father Farina says that the only true influence we have on people is through supernatural love. This sanctity (not an obnoxious piety) so affects others that they can be saved by it. Even though we *seem* to increase the delinquency of others (and we have been many a time charged with it), we can do for others, through God's grace, what no law enforcement can do, what no common sense can achieve. Father Farina extols love in all his conferences, and stresses the agonies through which one must pass to attain it.

Father de Montcheuil wrote magnificently on freedom, that tremendous gift of God Who desires that we love Him freely and desires this love so intensely that He gave His only begotten Son for us. Love and Freedom—they are great and noble words. But we learn about them, they grow in us in the little ways I am writing about, through community, through the heart-rending and soul-searing experiences, as well as the joyful ones, which we have in living together.

And so I firmly believe, I have faith, that Maurice O'Connell, in addition to being a kind friend who built the furniture of our chapel and some barracks for our families, who sat and fed the birds and talked kindly to the children on the sunny steps before his little house, was an instrument chosen by God to make us grow in wisdom and faith and love.

God rewarded him at the end. He was quite conscious when he received the great sacrament of the Church, extreme unction; he was surrounded by little children to the last; and even at his grave he had the prayers of kind friends. He had all that any Pope or king could receive at the hands of the Church, a Christian burial, in consecrated ground. May he rest in peace.

A group at Easton farm.
Mr. O'Connell stands at far right;
Peter Maurin sits in front, center.

Chapter 5

The War Years

THOUGH THE WAR WAS A DIFFICULT TIME FOR ALL OF THE HOUSES of hospitality, and ours was no exception, somehow we got through it on Mott Street. Our pacifist position made matters no easier. We once went so far as to print a box in *The Catholic Worker* urging men not to register for the draft. This evidently was considered as having gone too far, for I was called to the Chancery and told, "Dorothy, you must stand corrected." I was not quite sure what that meant, but I did assent, because I realized that one should not tell another what to do in such circumstances. We had to follow our own consciences, which later took us to jail; but our work in getting out a paper was an attempt to arouse the conscience of others, not to advise action for which they were not prepared.

Our own "war effort," as the saying goes, consisted largely of providing a refuge for the seamen of the merchant marine.

Many of those who came ashore were met by thieves in the guise of friends, who fed them doped liquor and robbed them of all they had, even their clothes. It was too well known that they received large bonuses for sailing through mined waters, and the jackals were lying in wait for them. Only looking for a good time, they did not seem to realize how dangerous a pursuit this can be along the New York waterfront and the Bowery.

It never ceased to grieve me how quickly men could lose their dignity when they were down-and-out in this way. As members of a group, as union men on strike, they could endure poverty and privation. But to be forced to go on a breadline or to go to a mission for the bare necessities made them feel completely degraded. For this reason, we never asked any questions of these wounded ones, never checked with any agencies as to help previously received. We only tried to fulfill their immediate needs without probing, and to make them feel at home, and try to help them in regaining some measure of self-respect. As the war went on, some friends we saw no more. We learned that one had been torpedoed and died in an open boat after enduring for days the torture of hunger and thirst.

To keep the house going we had only those who were too ill or too old to come under the draft or to go to conscientious objector camps. Making matters worse, Peter fell ill at this time and had to be cared for like a child. But we did have a tower of strength in this trying period: a large, slow-moving friend named David Mason who had been a proofreader on a Philadelphia newspaper. He had also run the house of hospitality in Philadelphia, and came to us after it was closed down by the war. David had charge of cooking and of running the house; then, as we were drained gradually of more active younger men, he took over the job of getting out the paper. No crisis was too much for him, and there were many of them.

Then one day two FBI men came in and asked for him. An old man who sat around all day listening to symphonies on the radio amiably directed them to the kitchen upstairs. There they found David, a large woman's apron around him making fruit gelatine for supper. It turned out that, although he was forty-five, just a few months within draft age, he had not bothered to register, even as a conscientious objector.

The men placed him under arrest and took him to a detention house on West Street. He was not at all averse to being confined, for he had been looking forward to a time of irresponsibility in which he could indulge himself by writing a long-planned novel. His only complaint was directed at the Jello, which, he said, had the consistency of a rubber ball. When his case came up, the judge released him on sight. So, after a week's absence, to our great relief and joy David was back with us again—cooking, writing, editing, and, in his spare moments, inventing. (He was at that time trying to construct a Chinese typewriter, a pursuit that brought cries of outrage from the destitute, who claimed that his workshop took up space that might have housed three men.)

Other houses of hospitality were having their troubles, too, as indicated by this letter I came across recently in our files:

I heard about the Milwaukee house closing. The decision was made, I know, after much prayer and mental anguish. The girls there have been going through a lot of late. [The men had been drafted or gone to conscientious objectors camps]. . . . trying to do what is right and not seeing everything clearly. . . .

All this talk sounds grim and I write this with a heavy heart. Something I had, and others too, I guess, is gone forever. Damn war! Damn Pacifism and stands! I think I miss the peace, the tranquility of order within the C.W.—more than the peace of Munich that went with Munich. Somewhere along the line it went. Now there is—at least in some circles—uncertainty and confusion to take its place. One of the saddest parts of the whole business is the knowledge that there is no coming back—it is all over—to the warmth and understanding we once knew together. Profound disagreement is a wall between people and it rears higher every day.

How I wish you weren't a heretic! And sometimes how I wish that I were one too. But to agree with you means cutting myself off from a much larger world and that pain is one you must know well, so that my anguish of separation is meager in comparison.

Please pray for me—and I don't mean that as an apt or pious phrase to close a letter. I need some of your spiritual strength. One by one the boys have gone. First Jim, and, this morning, Tom. Now I who was to have been first am last. It will be a new world to face—new attitudes, new viewpoints. I wouldn't be half so grim about it could I bring the C.W. with me—but I can't."

Letters like this—word of more houses closing down—laid a heavier burden on our hearts.

But our life was not all dark. What a variety of visitors we had, and what a fund of laughter in the stories with which they used to lighten the hours! I remember particularly a Dr. Koiransky, one of our Russian friends, who was always ready to care for our sick. He liked to tell of going with his friend Irinar

Dzarjevsky to the house of Salama, another Russian, down by the Delaware Water Gap. There the three exiles hoisted an old car to the top of a tree and so had a tree house for themselves, where they could talk and drink vodka for hours on end and get away from the women. I could imagine the tumult they must have made, with Irinar, the basso profundo as he called himself, singing with Salama, the tenor, as they passed the bottle around.

In spite of rationing we continued somehow to serve coffee (with sugar) and stew (with meat), although many commodities were hard to come by. We had barely enough money to get along on, and no extras. Any inroad on our funds could be tragic —such as the incident of Gerry Shaughnessy and the wine barrel. Every fall the smell of grapes and of fermenting wine filled the neighborhood, just as the smell of burning leaves marks the season in the suburbs. The tempting aroma was too much for Gerry. He got into the cellar of the house next door and tapped a large cask of wine which our Italian neighbors were making. He kept on drinking, sitting by the wine keg until he fell asleep. The wine leaked out slowly and covered the floor. So we, the benefactors of the undeserving poor, had to pay for this carouse which no one shared, and no one except Gerry enjoyed.

By the end of the thirties and the beginning of the war years, the period of burgeoning growth of the houses of hospitality came to a close. One reason for this was the drain on our manpower by the draft and by the conscientious objector camps.

These camps—they were called Civilian Public Service camps— were really started by the Quakers, Mennonites, and Brethren, the traditional peace churches. They wanted to make a demonstration of "going the second mile" with the government as they called it, and offered civilian service instead of war service. The old Civilian Conservation Corps camps had been used in the time of the depression for the young men and teenagers who could not get work; they did a noble job of planting and reforesting and fire fighting and so on. These camp buildings were still there, and the peace churches took them over from the government. The C.O.'s were supposed to pay thirty-five dollars a month for board and room, accept conscription to the camps, and work for the government at peacetime jobs.

Dwight Larrowe and Joe Zarrella and a few others thought that we should have a Catholic camp, so we took over one at Stoddard, New Hampshire. At first the boys themselves did the cooking. Then Edna Hower, a real New England housewife, whom I had met while she was running a bookshop on the West Coast, volunteered to cook for a year. Then began the era of apple dumplings, apple strudle, apple fritters, applesauce, apple pie. The camp was in the middle of an apple orchard and nothing went to waste. The fellows even sat around at night and sliced apples for drying so that they could be assured of their diet of apple pies for the duration.

Edna had a runt of a pig given by some neighboring farmer. At first it used to run around the kitchen and snuffle at everyone's ankles. A few months later, it was already a huge porker and ready to be slaughtered. Of course they did manage to have meat, but it was never two or three times a day. There were two camps in New Hampshire, and Bishop Peterson was very friendly and gave us help every now and then. But the Army did not think so highly of the camp. It was the food that seemed to bother them, not having meat. The camps were closed down and the boys went to other camps around the country. Some of them went into hospitals to work as orderlies, male nurses, and anesthetists; still others worked in mental hospitals and homes for the feeble-minded. They did all this without pay, and, in fact, were expected to pay for their keep.

They had four long, weary years of this, working twelve hours a day sometimes and saving up their days off so that at the end of the month they could have four days in a nearby city. No pay, no honor, and—for the first year—not enough food.

Part II

Poverty
and
Precarity

< *Siloe House, a large building at rear
of the present Chrystie Street hospice,
provides shelter against the cold
of the Bowery to men awaiting a meal.*

Chapter 6

The Faces of Poverty

POVERTY IS A STRANGE AND ELUSIVE THING. I HAVE TRIED TO WRITE about it, its joys and its sorrows, for thirty years now; and I could probably write about it for another thirty without conveying what I feel about it as well as I would like. I condemn poverty and I advocate it; poverty is simple and complex at once; it is a social phenomenon and a personal matter. Poverty is an elusive thing, and a paradoxical one.

We need always to be thinking and writing about it, for if we are not among its victims its reality fades from us. We must talk about poverty because people insulated by their own comfort lose sight of it. So many good souls who visit us tell us how they were brought up in poverty, but how, through hard work and cooperation, their parents managed to educate all the children— even raise up priests and nuns for the Church. They contend that healthful habits and a stable family situation enable people to escape from the poverty class, no matter how mean the slum they may once have been forced to live in. The argument runs, so why can't everybody do it? No, these people don't know about the poor. Their concept of poverty is of something as neat and well ordered as a nun's cell.

Poverty has many faces. People can, for example, be poor in space alone. Last month I talked to a man who lives in a four-room apartment with a wife, four children, and relatives besides. He has a regular job and can feed his family, but he is poor in light and air and space. We know what this can be. Once, at the Peter

Maurin Farm, every corner of the women's dormitory was occupied. When an extra visitor came she lived in the middle of the room.

Then there are those who live under outwardly decent economic circumstances but are forever on the fearful brink of financial disaster. During a visit to Georgia and South Carolina I saw the trailer camps around Augusta, near the hydrogen bomb plant. Families of construction workers who live on the move make up a considerable part of our great migrant population. They may have comfortable trailers, but they are poor in the other physical things necessary for a good life. No matter how high wages go, a sudden illness and an accumulation of doctor and hospital bills, for example, may mean a sudden plunge into destitution. Everybody so shudders at the idea of insecurity that fear of it causes people to succumb to its pressure, mentally as well as physically, until our hospitals all over the country are crowded. Here, indeed, is another face of poverty.

The merchant, counting his profits in pennies, the millionaire with his efficiency experts, have both learned how to amass wealth. By following their example, and given health of mind and body, there is no necessity for anyone, so they say, to be poor nowadays. But the fact remains that every house of hospitality is full, and we wish we had room for more. Families write us pitifully for help.

More obvious and familiar is the poverty of the slums. We live in such a slum. It is becoming ever more crowded with Puerto Ricans, who have the lowest wages in the city and do the hardest and most menial work. They have been undernourished through generations of exploitation and privation. We used to have a hard time getting rid of the small-size clothes which come in to The Catholic Worker. Those who eat steak and salads and keep their figures slim contribute clothes to us; and Anne Marie, who takes care of the clothes room for us, used to say, "Why is it always the poor who are fat? We never get enough clothes of a size to fit them." Some of the poor who come to us may be fat from the starches they eat, but the Puerto Rican poor are lean. The stock in the clothes room at St. Joseph's House moves more quickly now.

Not only are the Puerto Ricans underfed and underclothed; they are underhoused as well. Their families double up in vermin-ridden, dark, crowded tenements. And this problem is not confined to the Puerto Ricans, by any means. In this era of widely proclaimed prosperity, shelter, a basic need, is the hardest thing to come by in our city. When The Catholic Worker started back in 1933, it was possible to rent all the apartments you wanted. Anybody could have a home in the "old-law tenements," which, after all, had water and toilets, and could be heated quite well with gas or potbellied stoves. (Such heat was often more satisfactory than steam heat, which cooled off too early in the night or stayed on during warm spring or fall days.)

But housing reform has meant that thousands of the older buildings have been closed down rather than repaired and made suitable for occupancy, while the new housing has not sufficed to take care of the dispossessed people. Our municipal lodging houses are full of families, as well as single men who are unemployable or migrant; surviving old-law tenements are overcrowded as never before by the tremendous influx from those that have been torn down.

Years ago there was no problem in renting an apartment even if there were five children in the family. Now it is quite another story. Most young families we know in New York today have had to "buy" a place, seeking a down payment from bank loans, from the G.I. Bill of Rights, from relatives or friends, or, in some cases, with grim self-denial cutting out all nonessentials until the money for the down payment has been saved. The fact is we are no longer a nation of homeowners and apartment renters. We are a nation of people owning debts and mortgages, and so enslaved by these and by installment buying that families do indeed live in poverty, only poverty with a new face.

In front of me as I write is Fritz Eichenberg's picture of St. Vincent De Paul (Fritz, a Quaker, does the woodcuts in *The Catholic Worker*). He holds a chubby child in his arms, and a thin, pale child is clinging to him. Yes, the poor will always be with us—Our Lord told us that—and there will always be a need for our sharing, for stripping ourselves to help others. It is—and always will be—a lifetime job. But I am sure that God did not intend that there be so many poor. The class struggle is of *our* making and by *our* consent, not His, and we must do what we can to change it. This is why we at the *Worker* urge such measures as credit unions and cooperatives, leagues for mutual aid, voluntary land reforms and farming communes.

So many sins against the poor cry out to high heaven! One of the most deadly sins is to deprive the laborer of his hire. There is another: to instill in him paltry desires so compulsive that he is willing to sell his liberty and his honor to satisfy them. We are all guilty of concupiscence, but newspapers, radio, television, and battalions of advertising men (woe to that generation) deliberately stimulate our desires, the satisfaction of which so often means the deterioration of the family. Whatever we can do to combat these widespread social evils by combating their causes we must do. But above all the responsibility is a personal one. The message we have been given comes from the Cross.

In our country, we have revolted against the poverty and hunger of the world. Our response has been characteristically American: we have tried to clean up everything, build bigger and better shelters and hospitals. Here, hopefully, misery was to be cared for in an efficient and orderly way. Yes, we have tried to do much, with Holy Mother the State taking over more and more responsibility for the poor. But charity is only as warm as those who administer it. When bedspreads may not be ruffled by the crooked limbs of age and bedside tables will not hold the clutter of those who try to make a home around them with little possessions, we know that we are falling short in our care for others.

Chapter 7

The Insulted and the Injured

LAST WEEK, STOPPING TO BROWSE AS I PASSED A SECONDHAND bookstore on Fourth Avenue, I came across a battered old copy of Dostoevski's *The Insulted and the Injured*, a story which I had not read for many years. It was only twenty-five cents. I got it, and started reading it that very evening.

It is the story of a young author—it might be Dostoevski himself—of the success of his first book, and of how he read it aloud to his foster father. The father said, "It's simply a little story, but it wrings your heart. What's happening all around you grows easier to understand and to remember, and you learn that the most downtrodden, humblest man is a man, too, and a brother." I thought as I read those words, "That is why *I* write."

And that is why I set down the story I am going to tell now, the story of Felicia.

She came into St. Joseph's House one afternoon to see if we had any extra clothes. She needed a coat for herself and some things for her children. We had known her for several years. Felicia is twenty-two, a tall Puerto Rican colored girl; she would be very pretty if it were not for two front teeth missing. Her husband is also twenty-two. She had to grow up in a hurry, for she had her first baby, out of wedlock, when she was fourteen. At the hospital she lied about her age, and when she came out friends took her in with her baby. For the first two years she was able to keep him; then she lost her job and had to board him out. It wasn't until after she was married and had two more children that she was able to get him back.

By the time we met her, she'd been through a lot. Not long after she had the second baby, her husband lost a couple of fingers in the machine shop where he was working, and his mother agreed to take him in and the baby, too. But not Felicia. The woman had never wanted the marriage, and her house was already filled with eight people. Eight in four rooms. Felicia slept in the hall. That was when we first knew her. She was pregnant again, so she came to Peter Maurin Farm for a while. Then her husband got better and found another job, and they took a two-room apartment on Eldridge Street. It was hideous, scabrous. The plaster was falling off the walls; the toilets, located in the halls, were continually out of order, and the stairs smelled of rats and cats. The apartment she has now, she has told us, is much better. Her oldest child is seven. The others are one-and-a-half and two-and-a-half, and both are walking. You can see Felicia has some sense of dignity, now that she is a householder, with a place of her own.

She talked on and on the other afternoon, and finally stayed for supper. We had meatballs and spaghetti; afterward she got sick and could scarcely walk home. "Food doesn't seem to do me any good," she said. "I feel so heavy after eating I can't walk."

"But your husband's been looking after the children all afternoon," I protested. "You'd better be getting home!"

It turned out that, on the contrary, the seven-year-old was the baby sitter. "And her gas and electricity are turned off," somebody exclaimed. "There's an oil stove in the house—that's all the heat they have."

Aghast, we packed her off home, sending someone with her to carry her package of clothes. I had asked whether there was anything else she needed. She did not mention food or money or more clothes, but she looked wistfully at the radio which was playing in the room. She told me diffidently that if ever an extra one came in she'd love to have it. "You gotta stay in the house so much with the kids," she exclaimed. "I'd like to help my husband. He gets only thirty-five a week as a messenger, and I wish I could work. But there are no nurseries to take the babies—at least not until they are three years old. Tony's all right—he goes to school."

Later in the week, someone gave us a radio, and one cold sunny morning we brought it over to her. She and the children were keeping warm in the janitor's flat. The janitress didn't mind two extra kids; she had twelve of her own, eight of them still living at home. Since a lot of those were in school, it wasn't too crowded with a half-dozen kids running through the kitchen and living room. Every now and then one of them would fall asleep on the floor or bed—there were beds all over the place—and the others would play around them. Maybe they didn't make too much noise because they didn't eat too much. But the poor are like that. Always room, always enough for one more—everyone just takes a little less.

The children stayed downstairs while we went up to her apartment, taking the radio. We had forgotten that Felicia had no electricity, but here again we saw the generosity of the janitress. Her husband had put an extension wire up the air shaft from his own apartment to Felicia's kitchen; with a double socket we were able to connect the set and see that it played.

We sat down to talk a little, and in the quiet of her bare little apartment she told me the history of her furniture.

"How I got this place," she began, "it was this way. You know people don't like to rent to Puerto Ricans. So we have to hunt and hunt to find a place to live. This house has Italians and Jews, and we're the first Puerto Ricans. The place is all run down—as you can see—and nobody cares about anything as long as the rent is paid. Each apartment brings in twenty-eight dollars a month. There are four on a floor and seven floors to the house, walk-up. I'm lucky I'm on the third floor with the kids. Well, there was a woman living in the building, and when I was over at Eldridge Street in that two-room place she told me about this place. We were desperate. The water was frozen, the toilet was stopped up, so we had to move. She said, 'There's an empty place in the house where I live, where some friends of mine moved out.

It has my furniture in it. If you buy the furniture you can get the apartment. Twenty-three dollars a week.'

"My husband was getting thirty-five a week, and here we were going to have to pay twenty-three. Well, we have to move, that's all. So we signed a paper—that was last June—and moved in. From June to December 17 we paid her twenty-three dollars a week. And she paid the rent."

Felicia got up from the chair by the kitchen table (that table and four chairs were the only furniture in the room), and fetched a box from the kitchen shelf, full of papers and odds and ends. She began sorting through them. "These are my receipts for the statue of the Blessed Mother—you pay every week until you pay thirteen dollars and thirty-four cents and it takes twenty-five weeks. A store down on Chambers Street. And here are the receipts for the rent."

We began to look at them together. This, I said to myself, is how the poor exploit the poor. One set of immigrants exploiting the newest set of immigrants!

"I got sick in December," Felicia went on. She was coughing as she spoke. "Manuel had to stay home from work to take care of me and the children, so he didn't get any pay. She changed it then, this woman. She said I could pay her ten dollars a week for the furniture and then pay my own rent to the landlord when he came around. Now that is the way we do it. And here are those receipts." She tumbled more pieces of paper out on the table. They were all dated seven days apart; each testified to the fact that Felicia was paying ten dollars a week on the scrubby set of furnishings I saw around me.

In the front room there were a dresser and two overstuffed chairs and a davenport bed that another tenant had given her. There was a crib they had bought at a second-hand store; an ice-box, the old-fashioned kind into which you put a cake of ice when you have the money to buy it; and a combination coal-and-gas stove. However, the gas was turned off, the coal stove was full of holes, and the pipe to the chimney in back had fallen away.

I didn't look in the two bedrooms, but there was space for little more than the beds. They were in the rear, off the kitchen, and got air and a little light from an airshaft. Windows looked out on other windows; only by peering out and looking far up to the sky, four stories above, could one tell whether it was raining or the sun was shining. The rear room could be closed off from the other three and a door led into the hall, so, since there were toilets in the hall, one could rent such a room to another tenant. My first home in Manhattan, when I worked on the East Side for the New York *Call*, had been just such a rear room. But there it was warm; I had a white-covered featherbed and there was always the good smell of cooking in the house. Here there was no fire to cook by, and fire is twice bread, as the Arabs say.

I sat there with Felicia at her kitchen table and pondered the slips before me. For seven months she had put out $92 a month for rent and payment on the furniture. Since then she had paid $40 a month to the avaricious widow and $28 to the landlord, $68 in all, instead of $92—a generous reduction indeed!

"But this is terrible," I told her, frowning over the arithmetic.

"The furniture was pretty good when we moved in," Felicia explained, trying to account for the way she had been exploited and taken in. "It looked wonderful. You can't imagine how good it looked after Eldridge Street."

Well, perhaps it did. Having lived in Italian slums for many years, I knew how the housewives scrubbed and cleaned, and how they made everything shine with elbow grease and detergents. But Felicia had neither elbow grease nor money for soaps and cleansers. She probably wasn't very efficient about keeping a place up. After all, she was still young, and she had not had much experience, either.

"How much longer are you supposed to keep on paying?" I asked her, thinking of the papers she said she and her husband had signed. Probably it was all quite legal.

"We'll be finished a year from this June."

I gasped. Over a thousand dollars paid for junk; and nothing would be left of it by the time it was paid for. Enough money for a down payment, almost, on a house in the country.

While we were looking over the receipts, the gas and electric bill fell out. It was for $38.64. And how would that ever be paid?

I thought of a remark which Louis Murphy, head of the Detroit house of hospitality, was very fond of making. "It's expensive to be poor."

For some time as we talked I had been looking at an object hanging on the wall by the useless stove. Suddenly I saw what it was: a nylon shopping bag, the kind that bears heavy loads of groceries for shopping mothers without ripping at the seams, or giving way in the handles. Oh, the irony of that shopping bag—and no money with which to go shopping, and no stove to cook on either. No wonder she was sick, little Felicia, after eating meatballs and spaghetti on an empty stomach. She might well have felt heavy.

Never mind, Felicia, I thought to myself, as I went home. Spring is here, and you won't have to heat that apartment, or live with the smell of oil stoves. Soon a hot sun will be pouring into the dank canyons of the New York streets; the park benches will be crowded; and the children after the long winter can drink in the bright sunlight and fresh air.

Walking across the park, I saw the sycamore trees turning golden green and the buds bursting. Green veils the bushes around the housing projects people can't afford to live in. Even the grass is brightening and starting up from the brown city soil. The earth is alive, the trees are alive again. Oh, mysterious life and beauty of a tree!

Out in the woods of Staten Island (still a nickel on the ferry) there are birches, and beeches with their round gray bolls, the willows yellow-twigged, the pines bright green, the maples rosy even on a gray day. There is green moss in the swamps, and the spring peepers have started their haunting call. Skunk cabbages in all their glory of striped green and maroon have started up from the marshes and line the little brook at the foot of Peter Maurin Farm. Oh love, oh joy, oh spring, stirring in the heart. Things can't be so bad, if the sun shines. Oh, if you, Felicia, could be there. The ground is soft now, there is good dirt for children to dig in, and plenty of room for them to leap like the young goats on the farm next door. But in the country there are no houses for you, nor jobs for your husband. In the city there are houses—

shelter, such as they are—and there is human warmth, but the pavements are as hard as the greed of men, and there is no clean dirt for children, only men's filth. The country now is oh, joyfulness, and the city where Felicia lives is woe, woe and want. Never mind, Felicia, God is not mocked. He is our Father, and all men are brothers, so lift up your heart. It will not always be this way.

Chapter 8

A Baby Is Always Born with a Loaf of Bread Under Its Arm

THIS WAS THE CONSOLING REMARK MY BROTHER'S SPANISH MOTHER-in-law used to make when a new baby was about to arrive. It is this philosophy which makes it possible for people to endure a life of poverty.

"Just give me a chance," I hear people say. "Just let me get my debts paid. Just let me get a few of the things I need and then I'll begin to think of poverty and its rewards. Meanwhile, I've had nothing but." But these people do not understand the difference between inflicted poverty and voluntary poverty; between being the victims and the champions of poverty. I prefer to call the one kind *destitution*, reserving the word *poverty* for what St. Francis called "Lady Poverty."

We know the misery being poor can cause. St. Francis was "the little poor man" and none was more joyful than he; yet Francis began with tears, in fear and trembling, hiding out in a cave from his irate father. He appropriated some of his father's goods (which he considered his rightful inheritance) in order to repair a church and rectory where he meant to live. It was only later that he came to love Lady Poverty. Perhaps kissing the leper was the great step that freed him not only from fastidiousness and a fear of disease but from attachment to worldly goods as well.

It is hard to advocate poverty when a visitor tells you how he and his family lived in a basement room and did sweatshop work at night to make ends meet, then how the landlord came in and abused them for not paying promptly his exorbitant rent.

It is hard to advocate poverty when the back yard at Chrystie Street still has the furniture piled to one side that was put out on the street in a recent eviction from a tenement next door.

How can we say to such people, "Be glad and rejoice, for your reward is very great in Heaven," especially when we are living comfortably in a warm house and sitting down to a good table, and are clothed warmly? I had occasion to visit the City Shelter last month, where homeless families are cared for. I sat there for a couple of hours contemplating poverty and destitution in a family. Two of the children were asleep in the parents' arms and four others were sprawling against them. Another young couple were also waiting, the mother pregnant. I did not want to appear to be spying, since all I was there for was the latest news on apartment-finding possibilities for homeless families. So I made myself known to the young man in charge. He apologized for having let me sit there; he'd thought, he explained, that I was "just one of the clients."

Sometimes, as in St. Francis' case, freedom from fastidiousness and detachment from worldly things, can be attained in only one step. We would like to think this is often so. And yet the older I get the more I see that life is made up of many steps, and they are very small ones, not giant strides. I have "kissed a leper" not once but twice—consciously—yet I cannot say I am much the better for it.

The first time was early one morning on the steps of Precious Blood Church. A woman with cancer of the face was begging (beggars are allowed only in slums), and when I gave her money— which was no sacrifice on my part but merely passing on alms someone had given me—she tried to kiss my hand. The only thing I could do was to kiss her dirty old face with the gaping hole in it where an eye and a nose had been. It sounds like a heroic deed, but it was not. We get used to ugliness so quickly. What we avert our eyes from today can be borne tomorrow when we have learned a little more about love. Nurses know this, and so do mothers.

The second time I was refusing a bed to a drunken prostitute with a huge, toothless, rouged mouth, a nightmare of a mouth. She had been raising a disturbance in the house. I kept remembering how St. Thérèse of Lisieux said that when you had to say no, when you had to refuse anyone anything, you could at least do it so that the person went away a bit happier. I had to deny this woman a bed, and when she asked me to kiss her I did, and it was a loathsome thing, the way she did it. It was scarcely a mark of normal human affection.

We suffer these things and they fade from memory. But daily, hourly, to give up our own possessions and especially to subordinate our own impulses and wishes to others—these are hard, hard things; and I don't think they ever get any easier.

You can strip yourself, you can be stripped, but still you will reach out like an octopus to seek your own comfort, your untroubled time, your ease, your refreshment. It may mean books or music—the gratification of the inner senses—or it may mean food and drink, coffee and cigarettes. The one kind of giving up is no easier than the other.

Occasionally—often after reading the life of such a saint as Benedict Joseph Labre—we start thinking about poverty, about going out alone, living with the destitute, sleeping on park benches or in the city shelter, living in churches, sitting before the Blessed Sacrament as we see so many doing who come from the municipal lodging house or the Salvation Army around the corner. And when such thoughts come on warm spring days, when children are playing in the park and it is good to be out on the city streets, we know that we are only deceiving ourselves: for we are only dreaming of a form of luxury. What we want is the warm sun, and rest, and time to think and read, and freedom from the people who press in on us from early morning until late at night. No, it is not simple, this business of poverty.

Over and over again in the history of the Church the saints have emphasized voluntary poverty. Every religious community, begun in poverty and incredible hardship, but with a joyful acceptance of hardship by the rank-and-file priests, brothers, monks, or nuns who gave their youth and energy to good works, soon began to "thrive." Property was extended until holdings and buildings accumulated; and, although there is still individual poverty in the community, there is corporate wealth. It is hard to remain poor.

One way to keep poor is not to accept money which comes from defrauding the poor. Here is a story of St. Ignatius of Sardinia, a Capuchin recently canonized. Ignatius used to go out from his monastery with a sack to beg from the people of the town, but he would never go to a certain merchant who had built his fortune by defrauding the poor. Franchine, the rich man, fumed every time the saint passed his door. His concern, however, was not the loss of the opportunity to give alms but fear of public opinion. He complained at the friary, whereupon the Father Guardian ordered St. Ignatius to beg from the merchant the next time he went out.

"Very well," said Ignatius obediently. "If you wish it, Father, I will go, but I would not have the Capuchins dine on the blood of the poor."

The merchant received Ignatius with great flattery and gave him generous alms, asking him to come again in the future. But, as Ignatius was leaving the house with his sack on his shoulder, drops of blood began oozing from the sack. They trickled down on Franchine's doorstep and ran down through the street to the monastery. Everywhere Ignatius went a trail of blood followed him. When he arrived at the friary, he laid the sack at the Father Guardian's feet. "Here," Ignatius said, "is the blood of the poor."

This story appeared in the last column written by a great Catholic layman, a worker for social justice, F. P. Kenkel, editor of *Social Justice Review* in St. Louis (and always a friend of Peter Maurin's).

Mr. Kenkel's comment was that the universal crisis in the world today was created by love of money. "The Far East and the Near East [and he might have said all Latin America and Africa also] together constitute a great sack from which blood is oozing. The flow will not stop as long as our interests in these people are dominated largely by financial and economic considerations."

This and other facts seem to me to point more strongly than ever to the importance of voluntary poverty today. At least we can avoid being comfortable through the exploitation of others. And at least we can avoid physical wealth as the result of a war economy. There may be ever-improving standards of living in the United States, with every worker eventually owning his own home and driving his own car; but our whole modern economy is based on preparation for war, and this surely is one of the great arguments for poverty in our time. If the comfort one achieves results in the death of millions in the future, then that comfort shall be duly paid for. Indeed, to be literal, contributing to the war (misnamed "defense") effort is very difficult to avoid. If you work in a textile mill making cloth, or in a factory making dungarees or blankets, your work is still tied up with war. If you raise food or irrigate the land to raise food, you may be feeding troops or liberating others to serve as troops. If you ride a bus you are paying taxes. Whatever you buy is taxed, so that you are, in effect, helping to support the state's preparations for war exactly to the extent of your attachment to worldly things of whatever kind.

The act and spirit of giving are the best counter to the evil forces in the world today, and giving liberates the individual not only spiritually but materially. For, in a world enslavement through installment buying and mortgages, the only way to live in any true security is to live so close to the bottom that when you fall you do not have far to drop, you do not have much to lose.

And in a world of hates and fears, we can look to Peter Maurin's words for the liberation that love brings: "Voluntary poverty is the answer. We cannot see our brother in need without stripping ourselves. It is the only way we have of showing our love."

"Precarity," or precariousness, is an essential element in true voluntary poverty, a saintly French Canadian priest from Martinique has written us. "True poverty is rare," he writes. "Nowadays religious communities are good, I am sure, but they are mistaken about poverty. They accept, they admit, poverty on principle, but everything must be good and strong, buildings must be fireproof. Precarity is everywhere rejected, and precarity is an essential element of poverty. This has been forgotten. Here in our monastery we have precarity in everything except the Church.

"These last days our refectory was near collapsing. We have put several supplementary beams in place and thus it will last maybe two or three years more. Some day it will fall on our heads and that will be funny. Precarity enables us better to help the poor. When a community is always building and enlarging and embellishing, which is good in itself, there is nothing left over for the poor. We have no right to do so as long as there are slums and breadlines anywhere."

People ask, How does property fit in? Does one have a right to private property? St. Thomas Aquinas said that a certain amount of goods is necessary to live a good life. Eric Gill said that property is "proper" to man. Recent Popes have written at length how justice rather than charity should be sought for the worker. Unions still fight for better wages and hours, though I have come more and more to feel that that in itself is not the answer, in view of such factors as the steadily rising cost of living and dependence on war production.

Our experiences at The Catholic Worker have taught us much about the workings of poverty, precarity, and destitution. We go from day to day on these principles. After thirty years we still have our poverty, but very little destitution. I am afraid, alas, our standards are higher than they used to be. This is partly due to the war. The young men who came back and resumed work with The Catholic Worker were used to having meat two or three times a day. In the thirties we had it only two or three times a week.

This note from *The Catholic Worker* in the mid-thirties will give you an idea of what our situation was then:

The most extraordinary donation received during the course of the month—a crate of eggs, thirty dozen, shipped from Indiana by a Pullman conductor as a donation to the cause. God bless you, Mr. Greenen! The eggs we had been eating were all right scrambled, but they would not bear eating soft-boiled. They were rather sulphurous. Our friend, Mr. Minas, made them palatable by sprinkling red pepper over them plentifully, but we have not his oriental tastes. Fresh eggs! What a panegyric we could write on the subject! Soft-boiled for breakfast, with the morning paper and a symphony on the radio, preferably the first Brahms!

A christening feast which took place in The Catholic Worker office was positively an egg orgy to be alliterative. Dozens were consumed, with gusto, the guests coming from Brooklyn, the Bronx, and Manhattan, New Jersey and Long Island City, representing eight nationalities. Indeed if there had not been eggs there would have been no feast.

Again, thank you, Mr. Greenen!

I can remember how, when we were first starting to publish our paper, in an effort to achieve a little of the destitution of our neighbors we gave away our furniture and sat on boxes. But as fast as we gave things away people brought more. We gave blankets to needy families, and when we started our first house of hospitality people gathered together all the blankets we needed. We gave away food, and more food came in: exotic food, some of it—a haunch of venison from the Canadian Northwest, a can of oysters from Maryland, a container of honey from Illinois. Even now it comes in. We've even had salmon from Seattle, flown across the continent. No one working at The Catholic Worker gets a salary, so our readers feel called upon to give, and to help us keep the work going. We experience a poverty of another kind, a poverty of reputation. It is often said, with some scorn, "Why don't they get jobs and help the poor that way? Why are they begging and living off others?"

All I can say to such critics is that it would complicate things to give a salary to Charles or Ed or Arthur for working fourteen hours a day in the kitchen, clothes room, and office; to pay Deane or Jean or Dianne for running the women's house, for writing articles and answering letters all day and helping with the sick and the poor; and then have them all turn the money right back to support the work. Or, if we wanted to make our situation even more complicated, they might all go out and get jobs, and bring the money home to pay for their board and room and the salaries of others to run the house. It is simpler just to be poor. It is simpler to beg. The thing is not to hold on to anything.

The tragedy is, however, that we do, we all do hold on. We hold on to our books, radios, our tools such as typewriters, our clothes; and instead of rejoicing when they are taken from us, we lament. We protest when people take our time or our privacy. We are holding on to these "goods," also.

Attempting to live in the spirit of poverty certainly does not relieve us of the headaches of practical problems. Feeding hundreds

"Eat bread and salt and speak the truth,"
says a Russian proverb.

of people every day is no easy task, and just how to pay for the supply of food we need is an exercise in faith and hope.

The location of the house makes a difference, for one thing. In some cities the houses of hospitality got a great deal of food from restaurants and even hospitals. In New York City it is against the law to pick up such leftovers, however. This regulation goes pretty far, I sometimes think. A friend of ours, an airline hostess, marched in indignantly one day. "Our flight was canceled and here were a hundred chicken pies going to waste and when I asked for them for The Catholic Worker, they said no, it was against the law to give them away. They were all thrown out— to be fed to the pigs over in New Jersey! I guess the farmers must have the garbage can concession."

In the New York house we buy a great deal of coffee, sugar, milk, tea, and oleo. Our butcher is a friend who gives us meat at a very cheap price. We get free fish from the market—the tails and heads from swordfish after the steaks have been cut off. Every Friday we have chowder or baked fish. Sometimes there is enough for two days, Saturday as well as Friday. Occasionally, someone hands us sacks of rice, and then we have boiled rice for breakfast, which we serve like a cereal with sugar and skim milk.

But our problem is not just one of food. For the rents we must have cash. This comes to more than a thousand dollars a month, not to speak of taxes on the Staten Island farm, which are now fifteen hundred a year and going up all the time. Gas and electricity for a dozen apartments, as well as the house of hospitality, are especially heavy in winter.

In spring and fall we send out an appeal. We must give an accounting of this to the city: how much it costs to send out an appeal; how much comes in; how it is spent. Since no salaries are paid, and we in turn pay no city, state, or federal tax, our accounting is quite simple. How I rack my brains in March and October to talk about our needs so that our readers will be moved to help us! Sometimes, without embroidering it, I tell a true story of destitution, like that of Marie, who had been spending the nights with her husband on the fire escape of any old abandoned slum building until her approaching confinement made her come to us. Sometimes I talk about the soup line. But most often I retell Biblical stories, which are imbued with a grace that touches the heart and turns the eyes to God—the story of the importunate widow, of the friend who came to borrow an extra loaf for his guest, of Elias fed under the juniper tree, of Daniel fed in the lions' den.

Do we get much help from Catholic Charities? We are often asked this question. I can say only that it is not the Church or the state to which we turn when we ask for help in these appeals. Cardinal Spellman did not ask us to undertake this work, nor did the Mayor of New York. It just happened. It is the living from day to day, taking no thought for the morrow, seeing Christ in all who come to us, trying literally to follow the Gospel, that resulted in this work.

"Give to him that asketh of thee, and from him that would borrow of thee turn not away. . . . Love your enemies; do good to those who hate you, pray for those who persecute and calumniate you."

We do not ask church or state for help, but we ask individuals, those who have subscribed to *The Catholic Worker* and so are evidently interested in what we are doing, presumably willing and able to help. Many a priest and bishop sends help year after year. Somehow the dollars that come in cover current bills, help us to catch up with payments on back debts, and make it possible for us to keep on going. There is never anything left over, and we always have a few debts to keep us worrying, to make us more like the very poor we are trying to help. The wolf is not at the door, but he is trotting along beside us. We make friends with him, too, as St. Francis did. We pray for the help we need, and it comes.

Once we overdrew our account by $200. On the way home from the printers, where we had been putting the paper to bed, we stopped in Chinatown at the little Church of the Transfiguration and said a prayer to St. Joseph. When we got to the office a woman was waiting to visit with us. We served her tea and toast and presently she went on her way, leaving us a check for the exact amount of the overdraft. We had not mentioned our need.

What we pray for we receive, but of course many times when we ask help from our fellows we are refused. This is hard to take but we go on asking. Once, when an old journalist who had been staying with us was dying after a stroke, I asked a mutual acquaintance if he could give us money for sheets and find a bathrobe for the old man. He was the sick man's friend, but he told us, "He is no responsibility of mine."

But such experiences are balanced by heartening contrasts. On another occasion I told Michael Grace (I might as well mention his name) about a family which was in need; and he took care of that family for over a year, until the man of the house could have a painful but not too serious operation and so regain his strength to work again. I like to recall this because it did away with much of my class-war attitude.

St. John the Baptist, when asked what was to be done, said, "He that hath two coats let him give to him who hath none." And we must ask for greater things than immediate necessities. I believe that we should ask the rich to help the poor, as Vinoba Bhave does in India, but this is hard to do; we can only make it easier by practice. "Let your abundance supply their want," St. Paul says.

Easiest of all is to have so little, to have given away so much, that there is nothing left to give. But is this ever true? This point of view leads to endless discussions; but the principle remains the same. We *are* our brother's keeper. Whatever we have beyond our own needs belongs to the poor. If we sow sparingly we will reap sparingly. And it is sad but true that we must give far more than bread, than shelter.

If you are the weaker one in substance, in mental or physical health, then you must receive, too, with humility and a sense of brotherhood. I always admired that simplicity of Alyosha in *The Brothers Karamazov* which led him to accept quite simply the support he needed from the benefactors who took him in.

If we do give in this way, then the increase comes. There will be enough. Somehow we will survive; "The pot of meal shall not waste, nor the cruze of oil be diminished," for all our giving away the last bit of substance we have.

At the same time we must often be settling down happily to the cornmeal cakes, the last bit of food in the house, before the miracle of the increase comes about. Any large family knows these things—that somehow everything works out. It works out naturally and it works out religiously.

Dorothy Day and Peter
Maurin look over a copy
of The Catholic Worker
during Peter's last days
at Maryfarm, Newburgh,
N. Y.

This unusual picture of
Peter Maurin, taken at a time
when he was teaching French
in Chicago (a little-known
interlude in his years as an
itinerant workman), was sent
to Miss Day by the Maurin
family.

Part III

Those Who
Work Together

*Peter always enjoyed haranguing weekend
student visitors at the farm at Easton, Pa.*

Chapter 9

Peter Maurin, Personalist

WE LOVED HIM DEARLY, THIS PETER OF OURS, AND REVERED HIM as a saint, but we neglected him, too. He asked nothing for himself, so he got nothing.

When we all lived together under one roof in the houses of hospitality, he seldom had a room of his own. Returning from trips around the country, he never knew whether there would be a bed for him. The younger editors had their own desks and were jealous of their privacy. But Peter not only had no place to lay his head but had no place for his books and papers—aside from his capacious pockets. He had no chair, no place at table, no corner that was particularly his. He was a pilgrim and a stranger on earth, using the things of this world as though he used them not, availing himself of only what he needed and discarding all excess baggage. I think of him walking down the street slowly, leisurely, deep in thought, his hands clasped behind him. He paid no attention whatever to traffic lights; I suppose he put his faith in his guardian angel.

It took us a long time to pry Peter's story from him. Interested as he was chiefly in ideas, he seldom talked about himself. Only bit by bit and day by day were we able to gain any knowledge of his background.

He was born in a small village called Oultet in the southeastern part of France, in the Pyrenees. His mother died when he was nine, and his father remarried. Altogether, there were twenty-three children in the family. Occasionally, Peter would mention the communal aspects of their village; no doubt these influenced his life. The villagers had their own bake oven and a common mill to grind the flour. The Maurin family all lived together in a big stone house, in which the sheep occupied the ground floor. Peter was educated in the village school and went on to the Christian Brothers School in Paris, where he became a teacher. His sisters and brothers also became teachers. Some of them joined religious orders. At one time, Peter was a cocoa salesman in France. For a while he was associated with the pacifist political movement called *Le Sillon* (The Furrow) of which Marc Sangnier was the leader.

When Peter first came to this continent, he settled in western Canada, where he homesteaded. Later he wandered as an itinerant lumberjack. He came over the border into New York State illegally, and traveled all through the Eastern and Midwestern states, working in steel mills, in coal mines, on railroads; digging ditches and sewers or serving as janitor in city tenements.

Once, in Chicago, he started a language school in which he taught French. A picture of him taken then shows him as handsome, well-dressed, and apparently prosperous. Years afterward he sent this picture to his family, who in turn sent it to me. From something Peter once said I gathered that at this period in his life he was in love. But when we asked him whether he had ever married, he just said, "No."

Probably somewhere around the early twenties, he left Chicago and resumed his life on the road. This was his apostolate to the worker, the unskilled worker who labored with his hands. As Peter was fond of saying, he earned his living by the sweat of *his* brow, rather than by the sweat of someone else's brow.

In the years before he came to us he had been spending a good part of each winter as a watchman in a boys' camp near Mt. Tremper, New York, sleeping in the barn with the horses, mending the roads and cutting ice for the use of the camp in summer. He lived on vegetables and bread, and his little charge account at the village grocery never came to more than two or three dollars a week. If there was a conference in New York City he wished to attend, he would come. Sometimes the Monsignor, who had a parish there and who had started the camp, gave him his fare and allowed him a dollar a day on which to live. Sometimes he hitchhiked. He had access to the library, and it was there, in the seven years before I met him, that he evolved the ideas he brought to me. Slowly, I began to understand what Peter wanted:

We were to reach the people by practicing the works of mercy, which meant feeding the hungry, clothing the naked, visiting the prisoner, sheltering the harborless, and so on. We were to do this by being poor ourselves, giving everything we had; then others would give, too. Voluntary poverty and the works of mercy were the things he stressed above all. This was the core of his message. It had such appeal that it inspired us to action —action which certainly kept us busy and got us into all kinds of trouble besides.

"A spectacle to the world, to angels and to men . . . the off-scouring of all," St. Paul said, and that is what we became. The trouble was, we could not know when to stop, where to stop in our hospitality. Starting with Big Dan, with Margaret, with Mary, Stanley, Dorothy, and Tom, we soon began to have a community, and it was pretty much a community of the poor. People used to say, "With all those folks around, surely you ought to get more done; at least you could keep the place a little cleaner." But things didn't work out that way. What with people coming in for help, we were on the go from morning until night and soon did not have the time even to listen to Peter.

Peter tried to help with work around the place, but he was not too efficient. We heated the store and the apartment with stoves. The neighboring coal-and-ice man brought us chunks for our icebox in the kitchen and coal by the bushel.

Peter loved to build fires as he loved to mend chairs, but he did it so extravagantly that I wondered at him. First he would dump the expiring fire. Then he would throw in balls of paper, loosely bunched; then charcoal, or bits of broken-up boxes. Peter preferred charcoal. (Were there charcoal burners in the woods around Oultet? For me, burning charcoal smells of Italy and Mexico.) And then, on the sparkling bed of charcoal, some retrieved coals first, then the fresh.

By the time Peter was through he was puffing and panting—"like a water buffalo," John Cort used to say. Peter would stand there covered with ashes—ashes in his hair, ashes in his eyebrows, ashes in the creases of his face and ears, and ashes most especially on his broad shoulders and knees. If we did not clean him with a brush, he would remain that way to let the wind brush him and the rain cleanse him.

Once, Peter was helping scrub the office, down on his knees by the front door. Everyone who came in was a target for a few points on the dignity, the worth of toil—good for mind and soul and body, not to speak of beneficial in bringing order out of chaos.

Some manual labor every day—Peter felt the need of it. He liked to make schedules for himself and sometimes he kept them. But he was flexible; being a personalist, the human person came first. Here is one of his schedules for his life on a farming commune:

5-7	work in the fields
7-9	Mass
9-10	breakfast
10-11	lecture or discussion
11-2	rest or study
2-3	lecture or discussion
3-4	cold lunch
4-5	lesson in handicraft
5-8	work in the field
8-9	dinner
9-5	sleep

It looks so beautiful on paper, but it is so hard to live by. Any working woman knows how much time it takes to keep clean, to keep one's clothes in order. Peter was never troubled with such needs. Maybe when old Abbot Dunne of Gethsemane wrote me that he thought of The Catholic Worker as "a companion order in the world," he was thinking of Peter, its leader, who slept in his clothes, as the Trappists do, and regarded a bath as luxury. To the end of his life Peter tried to roll his trousers into a hard pillow around his shoes, so long had he slept in Bowery hotels, where only chicken wiring over the cubicles protected the sleepers from predatory neighbors, who fished for belongings at night.

When I wanted to talk to Peter about our work, uninterrupted by telephone calls or visitors, I often met him at St. Andrew's Church. Always he was attentive, reverent, devout, very quiet at Mass. It was not yet the time of the liturgical revival, when the faithful make responses to the priest. Then the Mass was offered in complete silence, the priest making his gestures of worship at the altar, kneeling, rising, holding his hands aloft, occasionally turning toward the congregation, exhorting them silently to follow him in his worship, his offering of sacrifice.

Very often in the course of our meetings I had complaints to make, discouragements to pour out. Peter would look at me with calm affection and in a few words speak of the principles involved, reminding me of the works of mercy, and of our role as servants who had to endure humbly and to serve faithfully.

He liked to talk of St. Vincent de Paul. When the film *Monsieur Vincent* came out, we all went to see it. The last lines of the saint to the young peasant sister were words we can never forget: "You must love them very much," Monsieur Vincent said of the poor, "to make them forgive the bread you give them."

We took those words to heart and tried to apply them to those who come to us helpless and in need. But it was harder to forgive each other—those of us who worked together.

Especially hard was it to forgive the pious, those who professed the Gospel, who were articulate about their faith, who went to daily Communion; and then came home to scoff, to repeat scandal, or to scorn the ideas and works of others. Some were truly mealy-mouthed Uriah Heeps, but others were gay scoundrels and one could not help but like them. How sad it is that the Esaus of this life should be so much more attractive than the Jacobs!

All kinds of tales are told about Peter. Once, when he had been invited to speak at a women's club in Westchester, the chair-woman phoned in alarm to find out why he had not appeared. I could only assure her that Peter, always faithful to his engagements, had departed on an early train. When I suggested she check the station, she replied that she had done so already and had found no one there except an old tramp asleep on a bench. "That," I said, "must be Peter." And it was.

Another story concerns a visit of Peter's to the home of the Catholic scholar and historian Carleton Hayes. The maid, thinking he must be the repairman, escorted him to the cellar to fix the oil burner.

Once, at St. Ambrose College in Davenport, Iowa, they awaited in vain the arrival of Peter as guest lecturer. Eventually they found him in the kitchen, being fed by a charitable lay brother who had mistaken him for some hungry knight of the road.

Peter's accent was an obstacle in the many schools and colleges where he went to speak. In the larger gatherings, students who could not understand him often talked and laughed during his lectures. But it was at the seminars, the smaller groups of teachers and priests, where Peter really shone. Once they could follow him, they listened to him spellbound, and many were influenced by his thought.

He always yearned for a large audience. Probably the only times he failed in his own immense respect for man's freedom was when he sought to sway the men in the breadline by playing records of his easy essays over and over while they waited for their soup. The idea that this was a form of "brainwashing" (a term which had not yet come into common usage), would have shocked him.

Writers have often described Peter as a nonstop talker. They have maintained that he never let anyone else get a word in edgewise, that it was never a dialogue with Peter but a monologue. I do not subscribe to this. Actually, Peter explained to us very carefully the technique he used to follow—on benches in Union Square, for example. First he (or the other fellow) would talk at length and say all he had to say. Then the listener had his turn to hold forth. To interrupt was a failure in technique. It was also to be understood that one really listened and did not spend the time while the other was talking in preparing one's own speech. Often I heard Peter say sadly, "You have not been listening to me. You've been thinking what *you* want to say." And unless one showed oneself properly contrite and willing to start over again, Peter would walk away to find another friendly adversary.

"I will give you a piece of my mind and you will give me a piece of your mind, and then we will both have more in our minds," he would say.

Joe, a wildly enthusiastic Italian boy who came to help us for several years, used to tear his hair over Peter. "He gives you a list of books to read," Joe would say "and then when you go to bed early so you can spend some time reading without interruption, he seeks you out and finds that a good chance to do some more indoctrinating."

(Joe was all for action. He was the kind who wanted to scrub and clean and mail out papers and visit the neighbors and help a family who was being evicted. When pretty girls came around to volunteer their services evenings he used to clap his hands to his forehead and say, "Heaven had better be good!" indicating the magnitude of the temptations that assailed him.)

Once, Peter came home from a lecture trip very hungry indeed; whether he had been to Albany, Pittsburgh, or Buffalo I don't remember. As he was eating ravenously, Joe looked at him and asked. "When did you eat last?"

Peter replied laconically, "Last night."

"What's the matter with you?"

"I didn't have any money. They just gave me my ticket."

Joe exploded. "Just because you talk voluntary poverty they think they can get away with handing you nothing; they think they're doing you a favor listening to you."

Peter then disclosed that he had a check in his pocket for twenty-five dollars. Even this did not mollify Joe.

"Yah," he jeered, "they give Arnold Lunn, the mountain climber, two hundred, or five hundred maybe, just because he is an Englishman and wears a dress suit. And they give you twenty-five!"

Peter was never easily put off. Following up his quarry, he would pull his glasses out of his pocket, set them on his nose, and start to read some telling excerpt from one of his favorite writers. He bought his glasses along the Bowery at the Thieves' Market. Sometimes they were just magnifying glasses in a cheap frame perched halfway down his nose. For a year or more he wore a pair which had one earpiece missing so that they sagged on one side of his face.

It never occurred to any of us to buy him a new pair—I suppose because none of us wore glasses yet. But, bad as they were, Peter's glasses never kept him from reading continuously and pestering us all with comments on what he read.

He was always trying to reinforce his words by dragging books and papers out of his pockets and pressing them upon people who seemed responsive. Among the books he was carrying one day was *The Thomistic Doctrine of the Common Good.* A cheerful, well-mannered woman who appeared interested in his ideas and eager to learn dropped in to pay a call and make a small contribution to the work. Peter immediately gave her the book. She returned it five years later, with the explanation that she had never had time to read it. As a result of experiences such as this, Peter took to copying out pertinent parts of any book that interested him. He would first read them aloud to us, then tack them up on the bulletin board.

Peter was an agitator and he left people agitated. I remember a lawyer who came up to me one time when I was speaking at the Cleveland House of Hospitality and said, "Peter tells me I should give up my practice here and go down to the heart of Arkansas, where there is segregation on the books and where they are proposing to sterilize the 'feeble-minded' as part of the solution to that problem." It might have been Mississippi or Alabama, but the fact that the lawyer was so terribly disturbed by this suggestion showed me what power Peter had over others. He not only made them think, but he even made them question their motives, their vocations. I felt this visitor was trying to say to me, "Am I practicing law to get rich or to serve my fellow man?"

Someone once described me in an interview as "authoritative." Later, listening to a tape recording of a talk I had given on the plight of agricultural workers, I had to admit that I did sound didactic. Since then I have tried to be more gentle in my approach to others, so as not to make them feel that I am resentful of their comfort when I speak of the misery of the needy and the groaning of the poor. But if I *am* didactic it is because Peter Maurin was my teacher, because he gave me principles to live by and lessons to study, and because I am so convinced of the rightness of his proposals that I have walked in this way now for more than thirty years.

"How can you be so sure?" Mike Wallace once asked me in a television interview. He spoke with wonder rather than irritation, because he felt my confidence was rooted in religion. I told him that unless I felt sure I would not speak at all. If I were ever visited by doubts—either religious ones or doubts about my vocation in this movement—I would accept it as a temptation, as a great suffering that I must share with so much of the world today.

Even then, deep within, I would be sure; even though I said to myself, "I believe because I want to believe, I hope because I want to hope, I love because I want to love." These very desires would be regarded by God as He regarded those of Daniel, who was called a man of desires, and whom He rewarded.

I was sure of Peter—sure that he was a saint and a great teacher—although, to be perfectly honest, I wondered if I really liked Peter sometimes. He was twenty years older than I, he spoke with an accent so thick it was hard to penetrate to the thought beneath, he had a one-track mind, he did not like music, he did not read Dickens or Dostoevski, and he did not bathe.

In the summer, or when he was ill, there were times when it was hard to be in the same room with him. Only when he was old and sick could we put him under the shower every Saturday and change his clothes and bedding and look after him as he should be looked after. I am sensitive about writing these things, but I feel I must point out that it was no natural "liking" that made me hold Peter in reverent esteem and and gave me confidence that all I learned from him was sound, and that the program he laid down for us was the right one for our time.

If Peter resembled a St. Benedict Joseph Labre, that too was a lesson for the rest of us, who spend so much time keeping clean, changing and looking after our clothes, taking care of the perishable body to the neglect of mind and soul.

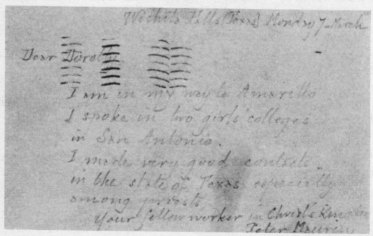

Chapter 10

Picture of a Prophet

AMMON HENNACY CAME TO US IN 1952, WHEN WE WERE LIVING IN the house at 223 Chrystie Street; and he left us a couple of years ago to go to Salt Lake City. But in the time that he was with us he made his mark. The men around The Catholic Worker look up to Ammon for his readiness to go all out for his beliefs—for his fasting as a means of protest, for the many days he has spent in jail, for his refusal to pay income tax because so much of it goes for war.

As I write about Ammon now, on August 4, he is very much in my mind. Two days from now he will begin his fast—that is, his long yearly fast. (He undergoes a routine complete fast every Friday as a matter of health and discipline.) His long fast begins on the Feast of the Transfiguration, which is also the anniversary of our dropping the first atom bomb on Hiroshima. The world had had obliteration bombings before, in which entire cities had been set aflame, but this one surpassed them all in horror.

For each year that passes since Hiroshima, Ammon extends his fast by one day. This time his fast will continue for fifteen days. During this period he will picket the income tax office, giving out literature and carrying a sign as a protest against the income tax, because 83 per cent of it goes for war purposes. "If we pay taxes," he says simply, "we pay for the bomb."

Ammon's example is particularly pertinent, for as I write this we live in a state of uneasy coexistence, filled with talk of limited

...tion to attack; and the more dreadful the imple-
...ar we manufacture, the greater our fear of attack.
...es as "We have to get our licks in first"; "defense is
...gh"; "to be strong and always ready is the only de-
...are heard on every side.

We hear impatient mothers say, "I'll kill you! I'll break your neck." The irritation, the edgy attitude of grownups, must make children think very early that they are living in a hostile world. The other day I heard a father shout out the window to his small son, "Wade into 'em! Kick 'em in the groin!" and then mutter apologetically, "Gotta teach 'em to defend themselves." Ammon was always one who stressed the necessity for teaching nonviolent resistance, instead of emphasizing man's right to defend himself. He understood it and he practiced it.

Oh, he is right, irritatingly right, although it must be admitted that he is often hard to take. No one else I know, however, seems capable of putting forth the sustained effort, and of demonstrating the tenacity of purpose so needed in this time.

Most of us are inclined to shrug and say with St. Teresa of Avila, "All times are dangerous times," and to settle down to our daily affairs, trusting God to take care of everything. So long as we say a few prayers each day, get to Mass, and go on living our comfortable lives, we feel secure because we have "faith." To Ammon, all of one's life is a precarious time.

I feel free to write with complete frankness about Ammon because I know he will not object. Many people consider him egotistical and self-centered, and so he is, in a way—enough so that he will appreciate my writing about him, rather than not. Ammon would prefer having people speak of him adversely to their not mentioning him at all. Hatred or love he can accept, but indifference, no.

Ammon wants to be paid attention to because he has a message; he considers himself a prophet. His sense of mission leads him constantly to talk about what he is doing, yet this is combined with a kind of humility, as though he were saying, "See what one man of reasonable strength and intelligence can do. I did this, I did that. This is the way I meet a crisis. Now, if we all did it together, we would ride out the gale, we would come through safely."

We call Ammon our American peasant, just as Peter Maurin was our French peasant. He was born in a tiny mining town in southern Ohio (pronounced "O-hi-a") near the Pennsylvania and West Virginia borders. His grandfather was a farmer, and his father the mayor of the town; and as a boy Ammon worked on their farm. When he was a young man, he drove Mother Jones, the pioneer woman labor leader, in a horse and buggy to a meeting of miners in Cannelton, West Virginia, only a few miles away. It was one of his earliest encounters with a radical. Despite a Baptist background, Ammon very early became an atheist and a socialist. Eugene Debs and Mother Jones were his idols. His principal beliefs were in trade unions and political action. He was a conscientious objector and was in Atlanta penitentiary in solitary confinement during World War I. Then he had only a Bible to read and became a religious pacifist. He was confirmed in his

Ammon gives an unidentified student a bit of his advice and enthusiasm. Meetings to organize Worker activities are, like this one, always crowded. Julian Beck, of The Living Theater, *is at far left.*

pacifism and anarchism when he read all of Tolstoi. From then on, guided by the Sermon on the Mount, he wanted to lead a life of poverty, loving-kindness, and peacefulness.

Farm-bred as he is, and so possessed of great endurance and vitality, Ammon is also a born salesman. He enjoys getting out on the street to sell, whether it be pamphlets, his book, or his ideas. This is his way of meeting a crisis.

I first met Ammon in Milwaukee where I was speaking at a big social action rally. The auditorium was almost as large as Madison Square Garden. I was the only woman on the platform. When the local Bishop had invited me to speak, I had asked if he was aware of our stand on the Spanish Civil War (which had ended shortly before). He said he was, so I spoke, bringing in our principles of nonviolence, the general strike, and non-payment of income tax as means to effect social change, as well as the voluntary poverty and manual labor Peter always stressed. Judging from the applause, I don't think the audience realized the implications of what I was saying. But Ammon did, and as I was getting into a car afterward to go to a friend's home for coffee, he squeezed in between me and a stout clubwoman prominent in Catholic circles, and started to talk at once—beginning, as he usually did, with the story of his life.

He wanted me to know that, though he was not a Catholic and thought the Catholic Church one of the most evil institutions in the world, he *was* a Tolstoian Christian, having become one in prison.

"And what jails have *you* been in and how long did *you* serve?" he wanted to know, to establish an intimacy between us at once. My record was modest: sixteen days in a Washington jail during the suffrage years, and a long weekend in a Chicago jail when they were raiding I.W.W. headquarters during the Palmer red raids in the post-World War I years.

Ammon clung to us all that evening. He was well acquainted, he informed me, with The Catholic Worker group in Milwaukee. He didn't think our people there had much gumption. None of them had ever been in jail. Ammon had been inside more than one jail. (It is easy to go to jail if you are poor. You can be sentenced for vagrancy, for sleeping on a park bench or in the subway, for begging, for selling neckties or toys on street corners without a license, even for walking through the park after midnight.)

Ammon has presented us all with a problem. What kind of work can we do for which we need not pay federal income tax? Even if we try not to pay it, there are the withholding tax and the hidden federal taxes on tobacco, liquor, the theater, etc.

Ammon found his solution first in working by the day in the Southwest. He irrigated, picked cotton, and did other farm work around Phoenix, Arizona, and was paid by the day. He lived, like the early Church fathers in the desert, on vegetables and bread. He sent his money to his two daughters, so that they could finish their education at Northwestern University's music school. He fulfilled his moral obligations, and his daughters were graduated. Then, when, in 1952, having become a Catholic, he came to New York and joined our staff, he worked for board and room, as the rest of us do, and so did not have to pay federal income tax here, either.

He has told his story in *The Autobiography of a Catholic Anarchist*, some of which was published in *The Catholic Worker* and which was printed as a book by the Libertarian Press, which supports another community of pacifists. He sold the book himself on the streets to visitors at our house of hospitality at our Friday-night meetings, and wherever he went on speaking trips. The sale of this book and what he received for his lectures paid his printer and gave him travel money.

He was still living with his wife when I met him in Milwaukee, and it was not until he was called upon to register for the draft, prior to World War II, that his wife left him and went west with the two children. Ammon said she was tired of the radical life. He followed her to Colorado, but she would not see him. He worked on a dairy farm for a while, until something I wrote in the paper about nonpayment of taxes struck him and he decided to go further south and work in Arizona as an agricultural laborer.

It was then he began to send me articles called "Life at Hard Labor."

Ammon is tall and angular. He lopes along city streets as though he were still striding by the irrigation ditches of the Southwest, where he has spent so many years. When his thick crop of wavy gray hair gets too long, it often stands straight up on end. If he's working at a sweaty job, he ties a blue or red handkerchief across his forehead, which then emphasizes how much he looks like an Indian. "We tend to look like those we love," Thomas Aquinas says, and Ammon loves the Indians, especially the Hopi. His blue eyes can be mournful or cheerful, but usually they are sharp and intent. He is straight-nosed, thin-lipped, and, until a few years ago, he had only one tooth. "Snaggle-toothed Hennacy" he used to call himself. One day a reader from Maine came into our office and, encountering Ammon, invited him to speak at a small college in his home town. The man was a dentist, and he offered to pull out the roots which remained in Ammon's jaw and supply him with an upper plate. A few months afterward, on a lecture trip around New England, Ammon stopped at our generous reader's office and without anesthetic (he scorns drugs) had the roots pulled and a new set of uppers made. He lectured the night of the operation. He remained just long enough to get his plate, and went on his way.

Today he is a handsome man, almost seventy but younger in his endurance and zest for work than many of the mid-twenty-year-olds around the office. It's a gift, a vocation, I tell him, so he ought not boast about it. He pooh-poohs physical disabilities and is a great believer in mind over matter and all the psychosomatic theories. He thinks, moreover, that everyone should be like him. I tell him we must have our Jeremiahs as well as our Davids.

Ammon is a vegetarian, but he says he doesn't "make a religion of it." He sees to it that he gets enough to eat: fruit in the morning, soup at noon, and a goodly meal of cheese, eggs, vegetables, and salad at night. Between times he doesn't scorn a wedge of pie and hot chocolate. Put him out on the desert and he would find some way to survive, even if it meant chopping mesquite and selling the wood from door to door in the nearest town. He has subsisted on the gleanings from the immense vegetable fields of the Southwest. Working in date orchards, he has lived on dates.

Someone who is always right, who points out that he knows how to work, that he knows how to eat, to fast, to sleep, to meet each and every problem of the day, can also be irksome. Yet Ammon's only two real faults are his too hasty judgments of others and his inability to see that he himself is ever wrong. His faults seem to be faults in speech rather than faults in action. "Do what he does and pay no attention to what he says," I often feel like declaring when he is guilty of some evident heresy or lack of charity. With most of us it just the opposite— we are so much better in our speech than in the way we act. In all that he does, Ammon is charity itself. When an extra bed was needed, he has given up his own over and over.

Ammon used to meet visitors at railroad and bus stations, and stay up nights to entertain them. He was always faithful in getting the mail and answering the telephone, and was regularly at his desk. He liked to have every moment accounted for. He spent the hours from eleven to three each day on the street, on Wall Street, around Forty-third and Lexington, at Fordham University (where he loved meeting priests and nuns), on Union Square, or in front of Cooper Union or the New School. When work was slack around the office, or rain kept him from going out on the streets, he set himself to indexing twenty-eight years of *The Catholic Worker*, binding five copies and sending one to the Library of Congress. When that job was finished, he started on a *Catholic Worker* reader, which ran into thousands of pages.

He has contacted countless people, face to face, with his good news of the possibility of the kingdom of God, where the lion may lie down with the lamb, where no man calls his cloak his own, where there is a companion for every weary mile. Ammon believes and acts on the belief that here and now is the time to begin.

It would take too long to explain his "anarchism," which is an individual brand. What he is really fighting is the modern state, and war, which many consider "the health of the state," to use

Randolph Bourne's phrase. He bandies about such words as "government," "authority," and "law" as though he would throw them all out the window.

Yet, if all men were like Ammon, there would be no need for courts, judges, or police. How strange it is that the anarchists I have met have been the most disciplined of men, lawful and orderly, while those who insist that discipline and order must prevail are those who, out of plain contrariness, would refuse to obey and are the ones most unable to regulate themselves.

The part Ammon has played more than any other is in fasting. Now, on the eve of his picketing, I know that he is girding himself for the ordeal. I remember how he did when he was with us. The night before, he took fruit juices and went to bed early. On Monday he was up for seven-o'clock Mass. He walked six blocks to Hudson and Houston, where he began to pace the street, carrying a poster and giving out literature. With a few moments of rest every hour, he picketed this way, every day except Saturday and Sunday (when offices are closed and no one is there to see him) for eight hours. As the days went by, his voice got weaker; when he came home he lay down on one of the long, low tables in the office to rest until he could regain enough strength to climb the four flights to his bed.

There were some days in which many cooperated with him; they took turns picketing with him, walking up and down, giving out papers, listening to the jeers of some of the men and women who went by, ready to shield him from a possible attack. (This last they have had to do on several occasions.)

Why picket as well as fast, some will ask? In a way it is easier to move than to sit still. It is easier to keep moving slowly, up and down the streets on a summer day, watching the traffic, talking to the passers-by, even if only exchanging a word. Fasting takes a terrific nervous toll, as I know from my own few experiences. One year Ammon announced that he was fasting until the crisis was over, but I talked him out of that, since we are perpetually in crisis. There is always one more crisis, but who knows which will be the one to precipitate war!

Ammon pickets the AEC in Las Vegas, Nov. 18, 1957.
The other man is the Deputy Director of the
Office of Test Information.

After Ammon had been with us seven years, he began talking nostalgically about going west again. While he was living in Phoenix, Arizona, we used to tease him about the effect he must be having on his fellow citizens there. "They are all Republicans," we told him. "They *like* your defiance, your refusal to pay taxes. What do your reasons matter to Barry Goldwater when you so brazenly defy the state and get away with it? You can do so only because it's a Republican town, where the rich are so rich that they know you will have no chance of making a dent in the social order. They are sure that your lone voice will not stop war or the profit system. But you will make no impression on New York."

Yet Ammon did make an impression on New York. Over the years he got a great deal of publicity. Characteristically, he pasted all the stories about himself into two or three large scrapbooks which he would take out and give to visitors, when there were too many of them for him to handle, or he was busy on the phone or at the typewriter. The *New York Times* and the *New York Post* gave space to some of his exploits. Like Barrie's Sentimental Tommy, he would crow, "Am I not a wonder?"

He liked women, too—especially young and pretty women—and greeted them all with a swift embrace when he met them. "I never remember the time I was not in love with some woman," he declared happily on the evening of his sixty-eighth birthday. Another time he said seriously, "There is only one woman I ever really loved and that is my wife." I suppose it was some aspect of his wife that he saw in all women.

His wife had tramped from one end of the country to the other with him, and they had worked together at all kinds of hard jobs. She left him when the two girls were eleven and twelve. He told me he cried himself to sleep at night, he missed them so. Yes, he has suffered. This marriage had been a common-law one, and I think he always felt free to marry again, although he spoke of his anarchism as an obstacle. He did not believe in getting permission to marry from the state by applying for a license. Anyway, until last year the matter never came up. Up to that time Ammon always had three or four good women friends who were truly devoted to him, even though he often spoke of women scornfully, insisting that they held men back in their radical careers.

Then, a year and a half ago, Mary Lathrop erupted into his—and our—life. She is a lively young woman who looks eighteen rather than twenty-eight, slim, beautifully built, with the strong legs of the dancer. She had worked for almost a year in a burlesque show. She told me once, "The chorus part was innocuous. It was only the strip tease that was vulgar. I guess I did it to shock my New England family, to get even with them, and also to get enough money to pay my psychiatrist. We practiced all morning, performed in the afternoon and evening, then went on the next morning to practice for the next week's show. It was a hard life. Many of the girls were supporting children."

Soon after Mary's arrival, Ammon got out of Sandstone prison, where he spent six months for trespassing on the Omaha missile base. After a speaking trip in the West, he returned to New York in time for the Civil Defense drill in City Hall Park. That was the first time a thousand or so joined the scant dozen of us who had made up the protesting party for the first four years. Some twenty people were arrested, not Deane Mowrer, Ammon, or myself, but among the twenty were three of our young friends—an artist, a stenographer, and a student from Baltimore who was visiting us. That night, when the women had been taken to the Women's House of Detention to start serving their five-day sentences, Ammon announced that he was going to picket all night along Greenwich Avenue, which fronts the jail. Mary said she would picket with him—and she did. She was always ready for an adventure.

She was getting rid of some of her driving energy, too. Ammon recognized that energy in her at once, and he loved it. Soon he began to talk of her as a wild young colt who needed to be hitched to a plow. He'd tame her, he seemed to imply. Certainly he began to work her hard. He was up every morning for seven o'clock Mass at old St. Patrick's Church on Mott Street. If Mary did not show up, he took to going to her apartment door (she shared two rooms with Judith and me) and waiting until she came out. They went for the mail together, and he kept her at the typewriter until every letter was answered. Around eleven each day they sold the paper on the streets and then went on to picket the Civil Defense headquarters or the Atomic Energy Commission. They would be back in the office for supper, perhaps, and out to more meetings in the evening. It was the kind of life that appealed to Mary.

"I like to be with Ammon," she said, "because I love to show off and so does he. I was brought up to show off," she added a little bitterly. She came from a broken home and spoke sadly of having two mothers and two fathers. She felt injured and aggrieved, but one could tell how much she loved her mother and father and how much she missed them. She turned to Ammon as to another father; she liked to cling to him. She was demonstrative, as was he; and he satisfied her need to show tenderness.

Sometimes she rebelled against his routine and morning after morning would take off to the flower market, where she begged armloads of flowers, with which she decorated statues, tables, and desks. We were in the loft on Spring Street when she first came to us. If she felt like running from end to end of the place, letting out Indian war whoops, she did it. (The loft was 180 feet long, so she had scope for her talents!) At other times she threw herself into skits or parodies with such verve and humor that we laughed until the tears came. Her imitation of Captain Ahab in *Moby Dick* and of a Southern senator were equally funny. But she could be as gentle and appealing as she was outrageous and boisterous. She has a lovely voice and often sings folk songs. Once, while we were driving somewhere together, I started reciting the "Veni Creator Spiritus." She began to weep. She wanted to join a convent immediately.

She used to paint pictures on the walls, on pieces of board she picked up on the street, on the head and footboard of an old bed she had rescued from a gutter. Her side of the room in our apartment was one grand clutter of murals, pictures, paints, paper, paint brushes, books, and clothes. Mary loved clothes. As fast as they came in to be donated to the poor, she dipped into them for a change of her own costume.

Ammon, like most men, preferred her in frilly things, her hair waved, face made up, and so on. He liked frivolity in women—but Mary rebelled at that, too, although half the time she fell in with his wishes. When she dressed as she pleased, she came either in rags or in some dramatic costume that set off her rather austere beauty. On the latter occasions she would put on a cultivated New England accent and the manner of the exclusive girls' school. I am sure that this charmed the Midwestern and Will Rogers type of person Ammon was. He liked to show her off to his friends.

"She's going out with me to Salt Lake City," he boasted. The boast became "And she wants to marry me." Not that he wanted to marry *her;* Mary wanted to marry him, he insisted. When Mary heard him say this, she would announce that what she really wanted was to go into a convent.

"But what convent will harbor that wild creature?" everyone around the office asked. "She frightens young men; convents are too conventional," an old friend of the family observed. So all agreed "she might as well marry Ammon." It was as casual as that.

He had been planning for a long time to go to Salt Lake City. After a few years in New York he had begun to miss the desert and the sky, the good hard labor and clean sweat. Perhaps he was taunting himself for giving up in practice his "Life at Hard Labor," as he used to call his column. People accused him of living by begging and talking rather than by work. (Writing and speaking are not looked on by the masses as work.) After five years, at any rate, he had had enough of New York. "I'll stay two more years, and then I'll go to Utah. There are fewer Catholics there than in any other state. However, I like the Mormons because they accept no aid from the government but have their own mutual aid."

He liked, too, the polygamous Mormons who defied the government and the concessions made by their own Church. Perhaps he was thinking of all the women friends he himself had.

Mary came into his life six months before his projected departure. The first plan was that she would go west and work with him. When it was pointed out to Ammon that this was somewhat unconventional, he decided he could forget his anarchist principles to the extent of getting the marriage license from the city. He knew being married by a priest was necessary, of course.

Difficulties began to arise with the chancery office. The Church moves slowly in such affairs. Neither Ammon nor Mary was willing to give up their companionship, although they were perfectly willing to remain celibate. So Mary followed Ammon to Salt Lake City. She worked with him, opening up a house of hospitality on Post Office Place, which they called the Joe Hill House and St. Joseph's Refuge. (Joe Hill was the Wobbly

[I.W.W.] organizer who was executed after he had been accused of shooting a man during a labor struggle years ago.) He named the house for St. Joseph, too, as a concession to Mary's piety. Ammon lived in the house, while Mary had a furnished room nearby and did housework to pay for it. Ammon took jobs unloading freight to keep things going. Like the Mormons, they gave up tea, coffee, and cigarettes.

Their "Gandhi-and-Mira" situation was not generally understood. In turn, they resented the bourgeois questioning of their relationship and stubbornly continued with it in spite of criticism from both Catholic and Mormon clergy.

All through the summer they worked in the orchards. From their letters it appears Ammon did most of the picking, while Mary sat by the irrigation ditches and taught the children of the Mexican workers to paint and make toys for themselves.

And then the winter came, and with the cold, indoor work. Mary's job as chambermaid in a rooming house was a hard one. She got up early each morning to go to Mass. The parish priest called her attention to the fact that she was out of place with the crowd of men who began to come around the little house of hospitality. He offered to give her carfare to San Francisco any time she wished to go. One day she got from him a bus ticket and an extra twenty-five dollars and—skipping the painful farewells—left early the next morning. She, who was a most devout convert, had fought with Ammon daily over his anticlericalism. So it should not have come as a surprise.

But for Ammon it was a shock and he was deeply hurt. He blamed me (because Mary regarded me as her mother), and he blamed the priest as well.

But there is always work to do. Three young men who were to be executed by the State of Utah needed Ammon's help. He joined in the plea for an appeal. He wrote and distributed leaflets, attended meetings, and picketed the prison. This work, and the job of running the house of hospitality, absorbed his days and his nights. He walked the streets, begging food to keep the house going. He even begged tobacco for the men, though he scorned such addiction himself.

Now the house is running full time, with as many as forty men finding some place to sleep on the floor of the large store each night. Ammon sleeps near the door, so that when he gets up in the night to let men in he does not have to stumble over anyone. There are Indians from the reservations, cowboys on their way to or from a spree, Basque sheepherders between jobs, and men off the freights (which come in at any hour of the night). The men are directed to Ammon for shelter; if they are sober, he lets them in. It is a question of the common good, he says. One night a drunken Mexican came, bringing a friend. "Don't take me," he said, "but take him." When his friend was given shelter, the man went lurching off down the street.

For a while Ammon used to write bitter letters to his Bishop, calling on him to speak out against capital punishment and injustice in general. I taxed him with being a most militant pacifist, and a most domineering anarchist. Now there are no more letters. His anger, which was never out of control before, has exhausted itself. He goes evenly on about his work.

At various times he has said he would move on, after a few years, to the West Coast, where his daughters are now living. But when I asked him in a recent letter if these were still his plans, he replied that he expected to end his life in Salt Lake City. He loves its beauty, he loves all that is good about the Mormons, and in time, I am sure, he will come to love the Bishop.

Chapter 11

Spiritual Advisors

DURING THE FIRST YEAR OF THE EXISTENCE OF THE CATHOLIC WORKER, Cardinal Hayes sent us a message through Monsignor Chidwick, then pastor of St. Agnes Church in New York. The Cardinal approved of our work, he said. It was understood that we would make mistakes; the important thing was not to persist in them.

And of course we have made mistakes. We have erred often in judgment and in our manner of writing and presenting the truth as we see it. I mean the truth about the temporal order in which we live and in which, as laymen, we must play our parts. I am not speaking of "truths of the faith," which we accept not only because they are reasonable to believe but because the Holy Mother Church has presented them to us. The Church is infallible when it deals with truths of the faith such as the dogma of the Immaculate Conception and the Assumption of the Blessed Virgin Mary. When it comes to concerns of the temporal order—capital vs. labor, for example—on all these matters the Church has not spoken infallibly. Here there is room for wide differences of opinion. We are often asked the question, "What does the Church think of our work and our radicalism?" The Church as such has never made any judgment on us. But individual churchmen, including bishops and archbishops, have occasionally expressed a definite point of view, sometimes in our favor and sometimes against us, though they have never stated their opinions publicly.

I have already mentioned the incident in which we "stood corrected" for publishing a box in *The Catholic Worker* urging men to refuse to register for the draft at the beginning of World War II. By way of contrast, illustrating the divergence of opinion among churchmen about temporal matters, I will mention that on the eve of the war Archbishop McNicholas, of Cincinnati, declared in a diocesan paper that he hoped that if America entered the conflict a mighty army of conscientious objectors would rise up. He contributed $300 to our first camp for conscientious objectors, and just before he died he sent us his blessing. (He made no public statements regarding war and peace after war broke out, however.) On the other hand, during the Spanish Civil War he had objected to our pacifism. He forbade any bundle circulation of *The Catholic Worker* in his diocese, although he did not object to his priests and people receiving copies of it individually. The paper, they were saying, was too controversial. A similar thing happened in Worcester, which was then part of the Springfield, Massachusetts, diocese. We had a house of hospitality in Worcester, but the priests were not encouraged by their bishop to visit it during that bitter civil war; and when a group wished to start a house in Providence, Rhode Island, the bishop there dissuaded them.

We never felt it was necessary to ask permission to perform the works of mercy. Our houses and farms were always started on our own responsibility, as a lay activity and not what is generally termed "Catholic Action." We could not ask diocesan authorities to be responsible for opinions expressed in *The Catholic Worker*, and they would have been held responsible, had we come under their formal auspices.

Controversy among Catholics revolved not only around our pacifism. When the CIO began organizing in the steel and textile industries, there was great opposition from the clergy on the ground that some of the union organizers were Communists. We were reporting the growth in unionism, and again our bundle circulation fell sharply, though not as drastically as when the Spanish Civil War broke out.

Our files are full of letters, on the other hand, from priests who have been with us from the beginning in our effort to advance social and racial justice. And only the other day we received a letter and check from the Apostolic Delegate from Rome, who is now stationed in Washington, D.C.

Our connections with particular members of the clergy have been very close and, I think, mutually rewarding. That with Father Conrad Hauser, S.J., was one of these. He came down to the Peter Maurin Farm for what was to be a one-day visit and stayed two months. The morning he arrived was bright and sunny, and Father Hauser fell in love with the place.

"I was a missionary in China," he said, over a second breakfast of coffee and toast, "and was kicked out of there. Until a few weeks ago, I was working in Haiti, and I've been kicked out of there. I mean, the powers-that-be down there wrote and asked my superiors in Montreal to recall me. I stopped over in New York, so I had to visit *The Catholic Worker*. I'd read it in China and in Haiti, and how could I be in this part of the world and not see you? And I'd like to see my Indians, too."

He was referring, as we discovered, to one of his early assignments in Canada. He had been stationed at an Indian mission on the St. Lawrence, among the Iroquois who, in the seventeenth century, had, with unspeakable tortures, martyred St. Isaac Jogues, St. Jean de Brébeuf, and many others. Now in the twentieth century they are highly skilled ironworkers, and more likely than not it is they whom we see clambering over the girders of the new skyscrapers rising in New York City.

"I'm a musician by training," Father Hauser said, "and I taught them Gregorian chants in their own language. I hear they live mostly in Brooklyn. I'd like very much to find them."

One of our staff people offered to accompany him to Brooklyn, but it was a fruitless search. The parish priest did not know their whereabouts; they had been scattered among some of the gigantic city parishes, which number from fifteen to twenty thousand souls. Father Hauser decided he wanted to stay with us for Lent. He loved the farm and he loved the people there. After a lifetime of obedience, and without having asked permission of his superiors, he suddenly announced that he would remain at the farm and say Mass for us each day.

Naturally, his superior in Montreal was curious about this peculiar behavior and sent his assistant provincial and a companion to Staten Island to call on us. I shall always remember (with much gratitude to God) the day the three Jesuits sat at the head of the table in the long dining room, facing our family, which numbered about twenty at the time. Among them were some old people, some withdrawn people, some talkative people, and, at the far end, a young girl who could only be described as "beat." With long black hair down over her shoulders, wearing tight black toreador pants and a man's white shirt, she was holding a baby on her knee. One of the young men at the farm was being very solicitous about her welfare. I shuddered to see him hanging over her, waiting on her, engrossed in her, quite oblivious of the three priests.

The three Jesuits, however—bless them—"had eyes and saw not," or if they did they understood. "They that be whole need not a physician, but they that are sick," Jesus had said, and their society was named for Him. I must confess that during their brief visit Father Hauser acted a little strange. He seemed curiously lighthearted and playful. We took him and the two other Jesuits down to the beach that afternoon. Freezing as the weather was, Father Hauser kicked off his shoes and socks and went wading in the calm but ice-cold bay.

Soon after the two official visitors returned to Montreal, I got a delicate, almost diffident, letter from the superior. Did I think Father Hauser was quite well? Yes, he could have permission to stay, but would I try to persuade him to have psychiatric help if he felt it was needed? They did not like to mention the subject to him, as they would not hurt his feelings for the world. Fortunately, Dr. Karl Stern, a psychiatrist from Montreal, who is also an author and a musician, was coming to see us a week later. I asked him to have a talk with Father Hauser. "One of the most wonderful priests I've known," he told me later, "but maybe just a little tired."

And who would not have been tired after the rigors of his missionary life all those years? I did not know his age, but he must have been seventy. His routine with us was a seven-o'clock

Mass, and since he liked to sing we had a sung Mass; he was most patient with our deficiencies in that respect. Sometimes he would turn around during the liturgy and translate a prayer for us with spontaneous enthusiasm. Once, when he was reading the last Gospel, "In the beginning was the Word," he turned at the end, with tears on his cheeks. "Do you know what it means to be called the children of God?" he exclaimed with joy. There was never a meal at which we did not have a little conference, but everything was so spontaneous, so cheerful, that no one had the feeling he was being preached at. Holy Week that year was a mixture of solemnity and joy. Soon afterward Father Hauser had to return to his work of giving retreats in Montreal. We hated to see him go.

It was not many months later that we got word of his death. After Mass one morning Father Hauser had suffered a heart attack. It was almost as though when he came to us he knew that his time on earth was drawing to a close and so gave that last gift of himself as a missionary to our group—a precious gift indeed.

There are many times when I grow impatient at the luxury of the Church, the building programs, the cost of the diocesan school system, and the conservatism of the hierarchy. But then I think of our priests. What would we do without them? They are so vital a part of our lives, standing by us as they do at birth, marriage, sickness, and death—at all the great and critical moments of our existence—but also daily bringing us the bread of life, our Lord Himself, to nourish us. "To whom else shall we go?" we say with St. Peter.

How much I owe to my early confessors! There was, first of all, Father Joseph Hyland, with whom my friend Sister Aloysia had put me in touch when I first wanted to become a Catholic. He was very shy with me—perhaps because he was young, not long ordained, perhaps also because of my radicalism—but he was patient and understanding and uncritical; he helped me to get through a difficult year.

The next priest I knew was Father Zachary, who was stationed at the little church of Our Lady of Guadalupe, on West Fourteenth Street. At the time my only job was with the Anti-Im-perialist League on Union Square, which was affiliated with the Communist party. Always, after he had given my penance and absolution, he would ask me, "Have you another job yet?"

He did not like my writing; he thought it was too grimly realistic. After he had prepared me for confirmation, he gave me Challoner's *Meditations* and *The Autobiography of the Little Flower* to read. I enjoyed the teachings in the little book of medi-tations but it took me years to appreciatae the Little Flower. I much preferred then to read about spectacular saints who were impossible to imitate. The message of Therese was too ob-viously meant for each one of us, confronting us with daily duties, simple and small, but constant.

When I moved to the East Side, I went to a Salesian priest, Father Zamien. It was he who urged me to go to daily Commun-ion. I had thought this was only for the old or the saintly, and I told him so. "Not at all," he said. "You go because you need food to nourish you for your pilgrimage on this earth. You need the strength, the grace, that the bread of life gives. Remember that Jesus said, 'For my flesh is meat indeed and my blood is drink indeed.'" This doctrine did not repel me, but it outraged my young brother, who called it cannibalism. "After all," I used to tell him, "we drink milk from the breast of our mother. We are nourished while we are in the womb by the blood of her heart. From her flesh and from her blood we grow before we enter into this life, and so from the Body and Blood of Jesus we are nour-ished for life eternal." We are shriven and we are nourished, and my gratitude for this tremendous gift only grows greater with the years.

Aside from the priests to whom I went mainly for confession, my first spiritual adviser was Father Joseph McSorley, a Paulist and a deeply spiritual and experienced priest. He had been the head of the American Paulist congregation, which was started by Isaac Thomas Hecker, a convert and formally a member of the Brook Farm Community at Concord, in the time of Emerson, Thoreau, and Alcott.

With Father McSorley you always felt that you had all the

time in the world. He would sit quietly, leaning his head on his hand, and listen to you. His technique—if you could call it that —was to be the nondirective counselor. I went to him also for confession when I had anything serious on my mind—or on my soul, I should say. I felt he was a saint, especially since he relieved me twice of grievous temptations. After confessing to him, I did not suffer from those particular troubles again.

Father McSorley was extraordinary, yet at the same time he was like thousands of other priests throughout the country, intent on their spiritual job. They were bogged down, perhaps, in temporal concerns, such as building schools and churches, but they were also the firm, strong timber and the solid stones in the building which is the Church. They never criticized others, although they did lay down strong and clear principles which by implication might be considered criticism. They encouraged the best there was in you and were silent about what they could not remedy. Above all, they left to laymen the concerns of laymen.

There have been so many priests who took time out of their vacations to visit us, and who have come to give us days of recollection and weeks of retreat, that it would be hard to list them all. But Father Pacifique Roy, a Josephite, is one who stands out. When he walked into our back kitchen on the second floor of the Mott Street tenement, he said he felt immediately at home. He was accustomed to living with the poor in the South, among whom he had done much of his work.

All that first morning Father Roy talked. Work was put aside as people gathered around to listen to him. The cooking had to go on, and the serving; visitors came and went, but we continued to listen. Father Roy, we soon realized, had the same direct approach to the problems of the day that we had. Wherever he was, he set out at once to better conditions, giving what he had in money and skill and spiritual help. St. Ignatius said, 'Love is an exchange of gifts.' To Father Roy the spiritual and the material gifts were inseparable. He went on to talk not about the social order but about love and holiness, without which man cannot see God. That day found him giving, and us receiving, a little "retreat." It was the retreat of Father Lacouture, his fellow French-Canadian, which had once inspired him as now he inspired us, so that we began "to see all things new."

Although he was stationed in Baltimore, he thought nothing of running up to New York on his day off. Many a day of recollection he gave us when we, in turn, went to Baltimore to visit him. He was a great believer in fasting on bread and water during these days, although the "water" at breakfast could consist of black coffee, which helped keep us awake during the conference. At the close of day, he would feast many of us down in the basement of the rectory, where the janitor, Mr. Green, used to cook up a good meal. One time we had roast groundhog!

In 1945, Father Roy got permission to come to stay with us at Maryfarm. There the first thing he did was to put in electricity, wiring the place with his own hands. Then he set himself and all other hands to digging ditches to bring water from the spring on the hill down to the barn (in which the kitchen was downstairs and the chapel, library, and dormitories were upstairs).

Father Roy slept in the men's upper dormitory with Peter Maurin, Duncan Chisholm, Hans Tunneson, Joe Cotter, old Mr. O'Connell, and I don't know how many others. They all loved him, with one exception. Mr. O'Connell, who was our collective trial, didn't love anyone. To put it charitably, he was perhaps going through "the dark night." All natural love seemed to be drained from him, as were piety and patience. One morning when we were singing Mass in the chapel, Mr. O'Connell began banging on the floor with his shoe, roaring for us to "cut out that noise!"

We had just started to sing the Mass and those first months must have been hard on Father Roy. He used to look wryly at the servers who sat on either side of him singing the Gloria out of tune. To Father Roy, Mass was truly the work of the day, and he spared no effort to make our worship as beautiful as possible. During even the coldest weather, when the water froze in the cruet and his hands became numb, he said Mass slowly, reverently, with a mind intent on the greatness, the awfulness of the Sacrifice.

To a priest who was complaining of his powerlessness to cope with the darkness of the times, Father Roy said courageously (it is hard to correct a fellow priest in so personal a matter) that if only he would stop gargling the words of the Mass in his throat in a parody of oral prayer he would at least be making a beginning.

To us he said repeatedly that when we had participated in this great work of the day we had done the most we could possibly do. One member of our community took this too much to heart. On days when Father Roy was away and we had no priest, this fellow worker used to tramp down and up the long hills to St. Joseph's Church, two miles away. Afterward, he would lie at his ease while the others—including his wife—chopped wood, carried water (the house was not piped), and did the work that meant food and warmth and shelter for him as well as for the community. He had done his work for the day, he said, carrying the spiritual burden for us all.

But Father Roy's Mass, once offered, did not prevent him from being a most diligent worker. He had what Peter Maurin called "a philosophy of labor." He took great joy in it, counting any day lost that did not see some heavy manual work performed. He felt he could not eat his bread without having shed some sweat. And if visitors and errands and other duties deterred him during the day, he would start in after supper, putting up shelves, hammering, sawing, finishing off some piece of work, going on until midnight.

Father Roy was a good-looking man—tall, lean, with warm and yet piercing eyes; slow, sure, meditative in his movements. He had good hands, well used to toil. I remember when I once cut my hand slicing bread, he laughed and said, "Rejoice in the Lord always!" Later he cut his own hand on the circular saw and had to drive himself, streaming with blood, to the hospital four miles away. I asked him when I returned from the city whether he had rejoiced. "I danced with joy," he said, "especially when they were sewing me up."

He liked to sing French folk songs. Once, with French discretion, he apologized for his "frivolity," justifying his singing by

*Father Roy at Maryfarm,
Easton, as he appeared
a few years before his death.*

saying, "One must reach people in many ways, you know." But he was more severe in some things than we were. He didn't like a radio in the house, and certainly he would never have allowed television. Both let in too much of the world. He loved parties, however, and we celebrated many feast days.

He also enjoyed going down to the chain stores on Saturday night to collect the leftovers which the countermen gave us free. When he had to pay for food, he'd buy pigs' feet or such cheap delicacies, although Eileen McCarthy, a teacher who visited us one winter, used to beg him for "a little of the pig higher up." She meant a ham, of course, but Father countered her Irish wit with some of his own; he brought her some pigs' tails.

Besides shopping he dug, he built, he all but started a lumber mill. One day, during his hour's meditation, as he sat with his eyes glued to the floor before him, it occurred to him that the boards of the barn floor, originally laid to accommodate farm trucks and tractors, were unnecessarily thick for a chapel and library. At the conclusion of his hour, he started tearing them up, leaving great chasms looking down to the depths of the former cow stalls below; It did not matter that a retreat was scheduled to start the following Friday night. There were still great gaps in the floor when the retreatants began to arrive. They were put to work nailing down the boards which had come back from the mill on the hill, sawed from the four-inch-thick flooring he had taken up. He doubled his supply of lumber by the move.

Hans Tunneson kept up with him in much of the work, although Hans was cooking and baking at the same time. Hans complained, however, that everything Father Roy built was geared to tall men—the sink was too high, the shelves too high, the tables and benches too high; even the toilet seats in the new outhouse which Father Roy built were too high! But his manifold accomplishments simply go to show how all-encompassing was his fatherly concern for us, how all-embracing his love.

Our life was indeed beautiful, with work, with song, with worship, with feastings and fastings. He was strict about the latter, however, and at times we sat down to the table with no more than cornmeal mush or oatmeal for supper. He ate it with us, he shared all our hardships, he rejoiced and sorrowed with us. He heard our confessions and he gave us the bread of life.

He also gave us conference after conference, and he gave the same conferences over and over again with the same enthusiasm. We didn't mind when he would insist that Father Onesimus Lacouture was the greatest preacher since St. Paul. We were used to enthusiasms that tended to exaggeration and hyperbole. We knew what he meant. He convinced us that God loved us and had so loved us that He gave His own Son, Who by His life and death sent forth a stream of grace that made us His brothers in grace, closer than blood brothers to Him and to each other. He made us know what love meant, and what the inevitable suffering of love meant. He taught us that when there were hatreds and rivalries among us, and bitterness and resentments, we were undergoing purifications, prunings, in order to bear a greater fruit of love. He made us feel the power of love, he made us keep our faith in the power of love.

Above all things in the natural order, he loved his active life of work. He had a passion for work—you could see it—just as Peter Maurin had a passion for thinking, for indoctrination. Both men were great teachers, who taught by their single-mindedness and the example of their own lives. And both had to pay the price.

One morning, not long after his return from extensive traveling and preaching in the South (it showed the greatness and wisdom of his superior that Father Roy was given such complete liberty), he got up to say Mass in our barn chapel. We were horrified to find him suddenly communicating right after the Sanctus bell, before he had consecrated the Host. By the vagueness of his words and gestures, we saw that something had happened. He might have had a slight stroke in his sleep which impaired his memory; it might have been a blood cot on the brain; none of us knew enough about these things. It was hard to get him to a doctor. What he wanted, he said, reverting to his childhood, was to go home. He wanted to go back to Montreal, where, in the bosom of his family, he could be diagnosed and treated. "Maybe I need to have the rest of my teeth pulled out," he said naïvely. (His nephew was a dentist and could do it.)

So one of the young men went with him by plane to his sister's home in Montreal. There was a long silence. The next thing we heard, he was in a hospital, the Hôtel Dieu, in the ward for mental patients. What had happened was that he had wandered away in northern Quebec and got lost. He was found in a tiny village, living with a priest and serving as an altar boy. The priest did not know Father Roy was a priest, too, dressed as he was in a suit over a pair of pajamas, but took him to be some poor man. (Mauriac said that Christ was a man so much like other men that it took the kiss of Judas to single him out.)

I went to see him in the mental hospital where, as is customary here in the States also, people who have lost their memories are confined. He remembered me, but not the others at the farm. He cried a little when he showed me the bruises on his face where one of the other patients, another priest, had struck him. He told me how an attendant, while changing his bed, had called him a dirty pig. He wept like a child and then suddenly smiled and said, "Rejoice!" I was crying too, and in our shared tears I felt free to ask him something I would never had said otherwise, feeling that it would be an unwarranted and most indelicate prying. "Are you . . . have you offered yourself," I asked, "as a victim?"

It was then that he said to me, "We are always saying to God things we don't really mean, and He takes us at our word. He really loves us and believes us."

Father Roy didn't have to stay in the hospital very long. He went home again to his dearly loved sister, who with her husband carefully watched over him. (His order always paid all his expenses.) Then an opportunity came for him to live in a retreat house for old and ill priests at Trois Rivières, Quebec, where, with the help and guidance of a brother priest, he was enabled to offer up once more the Holy Sacrifice of the Mass.

He had this joy for only two months, and then he became ill with what they took to be a slight case of grippe. Within less than a fortnight he died. He was fully conscious when he received the last rites of the Church; and he died, his sister wrote me, rejoicing.

Chapter 12

Editors Also Cook

THE CATHOLIC WORKER IS A PAPER, BUT IT IS ALSO A MOVEMENT.
On the one hand there are the editors, who are called "Catholic Workers." On the other hand, there are *The Catholic Worker* readers of the seventy thousand copies of the paper sent out each month all over the country and, indeed, all over the world. They may take violent issue with some article we print on disarmament, Cuba, pacifism, or the latest strike. When our readers agree with us, they are Catholic Workers. When they disagree, they are readers of *The Catholic Worker*. It is a fluid situation.

The editors are generally called the staff. But where does the staff begin and where does it leave off? Joe Motyka and Paul and Charlie, German George, Polish Walter, and Italian Mike are also staff, and as such play an essential part in getting the paper out. Since The Catholic Worker is also a movement, our editors and writers cook, clean, and wash dishes. They tend the sick, chauffeur the ailing to hospitals, and clean out vermin-ridden apartments; sometimes they decorate, carve, paint, play the guitar, and all of them join together in singing compline, the evening prayer of the Church, which brings the day to a close.

Now, in the year 1962, as I think over the names, I pause to ponder—why do people come? For a variety of reasons: some come to live their ideals; some come because they are just out of high school and college and are trying to find themselves; some come seeking excitement and adventure because they can no longer stand the monotony of their jobs.

Why do they leave? Some, to get married. The need to support a family sends them back to the humdrum work from which they have fled, but now, hopefully, with what Peter called a philosophy of work. The argument rages endlessly among staff and visitors: Can such work as filling perfume bottles on an assembly line, dreaming up advertising copy, or working in a bubble-gum factory be sanctified? (The fantastic terms that Catholics often use!) Some leave to live their faith in monastery or convent, to take up a life of service, to pursue a career, or simply to get away because they can't stand us any more. The reasons for leaving are as diverse as the reasons which prompt them to come.

Working with us has given many young men interested in labor and politics a springboard for professional work in their chosen field. Social work, editing, labor organizing and politics, teaching, writing, nursing—in all these active fields there are Catholic Workers or former Catholic Workers, and when I am travelling around the country I see them and their families. It is a movement of *men* because Peter Maurin set his seal upon the work. He was the thinker, the leader.

How much coming and going there is around The Catholic Worker! I remember one of the early editors left because I, as managing editor, refused to throw out another editor. Peter said, "No need to eliminate anyone, they eliminate themselves."

The opposite happened only recently. A couple of young "beats" moved in on us, living in our apartments, taking up the beds of the poor, eating the food of the poor, bringing in beer, women, and drugs in the name of their freedom. When they were asked to go, one of our editors left, too. We were being uncharitable, he said, with youthful zeal; we were being false to our principles. Didn't we say, or rather didn't we quote, "If anyone takes your cloak, give him your coat, too? Forgive seventy times seven."

It is a mystery to me how strange and unruly people become in the name of freedom. Had we been a Quaker group we would have had meetings, and tried to reach a unanimous agreement;

but, with one member dissenting, the situation could have dragged out indefinitely. As Peter said, we follow the Benedictine manner. One man is in charge of the house of hospitality, and what he says goes. His authority is accepted because he has won the respect of the others around him.

As for the paper itself—I am in charge of that—the masthead has seen plenty of changes. Years ago, when I put a man's name on who helped us in the business end of the work, an editorial worker announced that if this one's name was on he didn't want his own on, and in the ensuing dispute, which somehow involved everyone, *all* the names came off. Then last year we had so many listed as editors that Ammon Hennacy demanded that his own be taken off. Like Peter, he felt that "everyone's paper was no one's paper," and he preferred to be "on his own," the "one-man revolution." Stanley took his off because he disagreed on policy.

Why do people come and why do they go? Stanley, with his slightly sardonic humor, says, "They come with a shopping bag and go with trunks, not to speak of all the books lifted out of the library." Someone else sitting at the table says, "They come

The editorial office of The Catholic Worker,
on the third floor of the present Chrystie Street house.

with stars in their eyes and leave with curses on their lips." "I am going to write a story," Stanley continues, "about women who come to make over the farm and run it according to their ideas; and how, when they have made all the changes, they leave bitterly, saying how wonderful it was in the beginning." The Lord has His own ways of pushing people out of a work for which they are not suited.

Someone else contributes to the conversation by saying, "People come because they are in need of group therapy. Every malcontent Catholic sooner or later ends up at The Catholic Worker. There they see themselves in everyone else, and cure themselves."

There is no use trying to list them all. Who even knows which ones were the most important: Dan, who sold the paper on the streets; Slim Borne, who washes dishes; Arthur J. Lacey, who runs all the errands and serves in the clothes room; or those who could speak glowing words and write enthusiastically about work —while the others performed it?

The first of them all was Dorothy Weston, a dainty young Irish girl with black hair and bright blue eyes, just out of school. Her education was of the best: Sacred Heart Convent, where her sister was a nun; Fordham University; Columbia School of Journalism. She was more scholar than journalist, and when she prepared a paper on birth control or on the Ohrbach strike she made a thorough job of it.

She had an unfortunate habit of sleeping until noon, because she loved the quiet of night in which to work and read—as we all do—and, like most young ones, she hated getting up in the morning. At first she lived on West End Avenue, where her mother owned an apartment house, but eventually she came to spend full time with us. It was embarrassing to have a beautiful young creature asleep on a couch made up in the room in back of the office, her arms flung up on either side of her head, her black hair silhouetted against the pillow. Even with a screen around her, one could of course feel her presence; and the fellows who came in to help us had to go through the room to get to the kitchen for water or a midmorning cup of coffee. Later she married, and she lives in Europe now.

Then there was Eileen Corridon, a fierce worker like her cousin (the priest who was portrayed in the film *Waterfront*). She left to start a magazine of her own. And Frank O'Donnell, our first business manager, who left because of marriage and a growing family (for a long time afterward, though, Frank lived at The Catholic Worker farming commune at Upton, Massachusetts).

These were the first, and they in turn were helped by the unemployed who came in. There were the three Dans: Big Dan (of whom I have already written), and "Little Dan," a bookkeeper out of a job, and a brewery worker we called "Middle-Sized Dan." There were Larry Doyle, and Mary Sheehan, and Joe Bennett, my first fellow salesman, who died young of heart trouble.

Then, when we moved to our second home on West Charles Street, near the river, there were three other young men: Bill Callahan, Eddie Priest, and Jim Montague. Bill helped edit the paper; Eddie started our first small press for pamphlets; and Jim started the first farming commune, at Easton, Pennsylvania.

When we got the house on Mott Street, the most important workers were Gerry Griffin (an irascible, hard-working young man who endeared himself to me by loving Dostoevski), and Joe Zarrella; and it was a good ten years that they stuck by, with time out for the war, when they both drove ambulances in the American Field Service. Joe is married now; Gerry, a teacher at Queens College, is only now about to be married.

Julia Porcelli was one of the most responsible and hardworking girls we ever had. Beginning at the age of eighteen, she ran the women's house of hospitality and the children's camps, and worked in the office besides. Now she is wife, mother, and artist, and her life is fuller than ever.

John Cort, tall, blond, argumentative, not long out of Harvard, of a family of teachers and journalists, also came to us then, and was so interested in labor that it was through his efforts that a Catholic Association of Trade Unionists got under way, just before the CIO came into being. He and Bill Callahan and Joe Hughes and Charles O'Rourke were all active in the National

Maritime Union strike in 1936-37. They ran our West Side head-quarters, where we fed the striking men and kept a day-center open for three months. (See chapter 3.) When John Cort left the Worker he got a job with the Newspaper Guild in Boston. He is now advisor to the Peace Corps in the Philippines, where he has moved with wife and ten children. Jack Thornton and David Mason both came from Philadelphia to help us at the beginning of World War II, and when Jack was drafted, David, and Arthur Sheehan, from the Boston house of hospitality, took over the work, with the help of Smokey Joe and Duncan Chisholm.

The postwar group included Tom Sullivan, from the Chicago house of hospitality, and Jack English, from the Cleveland one. Both had been in the service, Tom in the Pacific area and Jack in a prisoner-of-war camp in Rumania (as gunner in a bomber he had been shot down). Tom is now teaching high school on Long Island, and Jack is a Trappist priest in Conyers, Georgia. Bob Ludlow was the one pacifist of that triumvirate, and heated discussions which began as friendly banter often ended in quiet but venomous words between one and another of them. But the three of them worked well together for years, running a good house of hospitality. Tom wrote a monthly column full of humor. Bob's articles on war and peace, capital and labor, and man and the state were so thoughtful and penetrating that they attracted the atten-tion of, and stirred controversy among, Catholic philosophers and theologians all over the country. He, too, has turned to teach-ing, the field for which he was trained.

There was also a grand group of young women with us at this period—Jane O'Donnell, who managed the farmhouse we had at Newburgh; and Irene Naughton and Helen Adler, who helped both on the farm and in the city as the need arose. Jane was beautiful, but was what John-the-farmer called a "commando." The men liked her because there was a great deal of fight in her. She was always undefeated in her opinion, battling cheerfully against heavy odds. She works now in an interracial parish with mothers and children, work which she dearly loves and which utilizes her great tenderness.

Irene, one of the brightest writers we ever had on the paper, wrote many keen analyses of unemployment, corruption in unions, chain store business techniques, and decentralization— to recall only a few of her articles. She had bright red hair and a warm laugh, and she could write nothing that did not have an Irish lilt to it, a poetic quality that enlivened even the dullest subject. She ran the women's floor in the house of hospitality, first when it occupied two apartments on the fifth floor of our house on Mott Street, and later on Chrystie Street. Her heart was torn between the needs of the old women from the Bowery and a young one with twins who stayed with us for a time. She found it painfully hard to divide herself and try to do justice to both kinds of work. I remember her coming in from the Bowery one night supporting the tottering steps of a little old lady called Elly, a habitué of Sammy's Bowery Follies who was quite drunk. Her speech was cultured, was Elly's (she said she had been educated in Paris), and she assured us she would indeed be saved in spite of her bad life because she had made a pilgrimage to the grave of the Little Flower, Therese Martin, and had sat there saying a rosary. She died peacefully with us a few years later. Helen, too, did everything from baking bread and writing articles to taking neighboring families on trips to clinics and to Coney Island. She left our work, finally, to take a course in practical nursing so she could be of more help to the poor. Helen was the one responsible for drawing Charles McCormack into the work.

Charles had used his G.I. Bill of Rights to take a business course, but as a salesman of what were then wire recorders he was not very happy. Passing by Corpus Christi Church one day, he dropped in for a visit and found there a copy of *The Catholic Worker*. It was near Columbia University, and when Father Ford was pastor, the paper, despite the controversial character of its articles, was always kept in the rear of the church, together with the *Catholic News* and the *Sunday Visitor*. It was the first time Charles had seen it, and he sat there and read it through. Then he took the subway to Canal Street to look us over. He was too shy to go in. "I went to the nearest tavern first and got a couple of beers," he said. When he finally made it to the office, Helen

Adler was the first person he encountered, and she happened to be full of enthusiasm for a retreat which was to begin the next day at our Newburgh farm. It was just the place for Charles, she decided, and he was easily persuaded to go.

He spent the summer making one retreat after the other, driving the station wagon on errands, picking up people at the train, and doing the shopping. For the last four of his six years with us, he was in charge of the work.

Bob Steed had come up from Memphis and was working with us at that time, and Ammon Hennacy had left his agricultural labor in the Southwest and had become a regular member of the staff, so once again we had a well-rounded crew.

Charles was one of the best to manage a household, however. He liked to go out after the furniture and clothing offered by our readers, taking many of the men of the house to help him. He visited the sick in the hospitals and no trip out to Brentwood or Central Islip was too much for him. He passed no judgments but kept good order in the house and the men respected him. And then suddenly fell in love with a doctor's secretary at Bellevue, and she with him. We had seen other romances budding and blossoming over the years, but this was sudden, and we were delighted with the unexpectedness of it. Bob and Ammon took over, and when they left others came, so the work goes on.

There is no end to the list of our editors, our fellow workers. And now, wherever one looks around the country—in the fields of social work, editing, labor organization, politics, teaching, writing, nursing, and others—one sees former Catholic Workers. If I am the mother and grandmother of a far-flung family, Peter's thought was the catalyst that brought it all about.

Marge Hughes is as much of a secretary as I have ever had. She first came in the early days of the work, when she was twenty-one, and helped me with our already enormous correspondence. She left to care for her home and four children, and then, when they were in their teens, she returned to us. Now she lives in one of the Staten Island beach houses—the other is mainly a summer refuge for Puerto Rican families.

In the early days she often accompanied Peter on his forays into public squares to recite his essays and provoke discussion. She was the only one among us brave enough to participate in Peter's one-and-only attempt at antiphonal chanting in Columbus Circle.

Marge also went along with Peter on a visit to Paul Tillich, the distinguished theologian, among others, to ask him for a brief summary of his thought. (Their idea was to popularize ideas through enlisting the cooperation of syndicated newspaper columnists and well-known political figures.) It is a measure of Tillich's greatness that he did his best to give them a one-page resumé. Alas, it is lost somewhere in the files, and therefore was never used as Peter had intended.

Marge was crazy about dancing. When she wasn't helping me or accompanying Peter, she was dancing all over the East Side, at the many taverns which made a specialty of folk music and folk dancing. Her companion on such expeditions to explore these aspects of "cult, culture, and cultivation" was a man named Leonard Austin, who was a great help to Peter in developing his intellectual synthesis. Everyone who came, whatever his interests, seemed to find a niche at The Catholic Worker. Marge is the epitome of hospitality. It is never too late or too early for her to be about, serving others. When there is nothing in the house but rice and a few vestiges of vegetables, she can produce a delicious dinner consisting mainly of fried rice and onions.

Hers is a joyous and uncomplaining spirit, never perturbed, always welcoming, when anyone from farm or city comes knocking on her door for a cup of coffee and an hour of good talk. Like the widow of Sarephta, she does not hesitate to use "the last of her meal and oil" for the needy and hungry guest, and somehow there is "always enough for one more."

And Stanley Vishnewski. I have a hard time classifying Stanley. It is now twenty-seven years since Stanley became associated with The Catholic Worker movement. He confesses ruefully that he has not yet made up his mind whether he is going to remain with us. "But fear of Dorothy Day drives me on!" he declares.

Stanley is one whom we call a "cradle Catholic." As such, he feels that we converts are rash and reckless in our radical stands and our picketing, in our pacifism and our anarchism. Stanley comes from a Lithuanian background and has persecution in his blood. He doesn't hate the Russians, but he harbors the resentment one might expect from anyone who has seen his native country dominated by a neighboring foreign power. This is an attitude which those of us converts who are of American Protestant background find hard to understand. We are used to being the dominating ones, not subject to others.

By now he has all kinds of tales as to how he came to be with the movement. His favorite version is that he encountered me one day in Union Square while I was lugging a heavy typewriter. He insists that he offered to carry it for me and that I replied, "Come, follow me." As he tells it, he says, "She was a little old lady, and I was a chivalrous young man—a knight for a Day." Then he adds, "I was seventeen and she was thirty-seven."

The truth of the matter is this. Stanley turned up in my office for the first time with a sheaf of poems. I had to tell him he was not a poet. His response was to put the poems away and start writing prose. By now he has produced a trunkful of books and stories, many of the latter published. He still hopes for the sight of his name on a book.

Stanley prints all manner of prayer cards for us, as well as reams of stationery and his own two-page tabloid bulletin called *The Right Spirit*.

He started by selling *The Catholic Worker* on the streets, and he kept at that until World War II. Then he began reconsidering his position. It was in his blood to follow the traditional teaching of the Church. He also believes that wars should be fought to defend the injured and to resist injustice—though he did try being a conscientious objector. He gave it up after four months in a camp for Catholic war resisters.

He still thinks in terms of the sword and white charger, though I believe the nearest he actually ever came to a horse was during a riot at the time of the National Biscuit Company strike. I was in danger of being pushed against the factory wall and crushed when Stanley interposed his body between mine and a policeman's horse.

Stanley has a wild sense of humor, calculated to delight some and rile others. When retreatants have come to our farm for spiritual exercises, Stanley has greeted them with "We rent out hair shirts during our retreats—specially made by Hart, Schaffner & Marx." He has been known to reassure our more conventional visitors by telling them, "We change our sheets every week—from one bed to another." Once, when a group of seminarians turned up, his first words were, "Oh, we always have plenty of room, provided you aren't superstitious and don't mind sleeping thirteen in a bed." He is fond of saying, "If all men carried their crosses, no woman would ever walk."

He loves to tell long stories to little children, who sit around him cross-legged on the floor. His most delightful story is a long one, the tale of "Oswald, the Hungry Lion." He tells it in the first person, and there is a great deal of repetition, so that when the children come to know it they repeat parts of it with him. When his jaws go round and round as he tells how Oswald chewed up various members of his family, the children's jaws go round and round, too. The story is so entertaining it took us years to realize it is a friendly satire directed against our pacifism.

Stanley cannot drive a car. He goes everywhere on a bicycle. One or another of the men on the farm is always borrowing it, so Stanley has to borrow it back again whenever he wants to use it. He is a Third Order Franciscan, although he does not attend the meetings, and has a large collection of books on St. Francis.

Some years ago a teacher, Gerda Blumenthal, chose as the subject of her talk at one of our Friday-night meetings "The Hero and the Saint." Sitting around afterward, discussing it over coffee, we decided that, among our staff members, Ammon Hennacy was "the Hero" and Charles Butterworth "the Saint." In more prosaic terms he is what you might call our business manager. A graduate of Harvard Law School, he has the difficult job of taking charge of the money and paying the bills. In the hullabaloo which is our office he is an island of quiet—a gentle, serious person and a very kind one. Everyone goes to him for help or advice, comfort or carfare.

For a long time it bothered Charles's conscience that he had not yet been to jail. Whenever a demonstration of civil disobedience against an air raid drill took place, he would debate with himself whether or not to participate. I urged him not to, on the grounds that we had to have someone left to take care of the office. Then, one morning some years ago, two men came in. They flashed cards showing they were from the FBI and said they were looking for a man named Jim who had deserted from the Army.

Jim happened, at that moment, to be helping out in our kitchen. Charles was not then in charge of the house; he was just doing general work in the office. I can see him now as I write, looking puzzled, not knowing quite what to do. Finally he went to find Bob Steed, who was in charge, but Bob was nowhere around. Charles then went back to the kitchen, where he found Jim, and told him that a couple of visitors whom he might not want to see were in the front office asking for him. Quick as a flash, Jim grabbed his coat and ran out.

Charles went back to the office. Because he is the most truthful of men, the expression on his face betrayed him. The FBI men informed him that he had committed a criminal offense, saying that they were going down to the Federal building to swear out a warrant for his arrest on two counts: harboring a deserter from the army and helping him to escape.

Some hours later they returned with their warrant. Charles, not yet having become articulate about his position, would only say that he believed people had to make up their own minds what they should do, and that The Catholic Worker was a sanctuary for people of all kinds.

For Charles, this was a serious matter. Arraigned in magistrate's court, he pleaded guilty, which meant he was a felon, and as such he would never be able to practice law. But perhaps, like St. Alphonsus Liguori, he had come to the conclusion that in a legal career he would not be likely to save his soul.

The case came to trial. Charles, in a quiet voice, read a short statement setting forth his beliefs. The judge kept looking at him amiably. At the end, he told Charles that his own son was a graduate of Fordham and that he was familiar with our work. He went on to say that since he had to judge by the law, and since Charles had pleaded guilty, he must sentence him to six months in prison. Then he suspended the sentence.

Charles has not been in jail yet. But he is a convicted felon, "for love of brother." He has been accounted "worthy to suffer," as the apostles were. The point Charles tried to make was that man, in liberty of spirit, must decide for himself. So far as he himself was concerned, he felt that by virtue of his position at The Catholic Worker he had to help those in need—no matter what that need was and whether or not it was through their own fault.

Deane Mowrer, one of our associate editors, is an all-out intellectual, widely read in literature, who once taught at the University of New Mexico. In addition to her articles on life at Peter Maurin Farm, she writes poetry—and very good poetry, too. Each year, except the first, six years ago, she has picketed with the rest of us against New York's compulsory air raid drills. Many times we have sat side by side in a cell awaiting trial, talking together, reading together.

Deane is on the farm now, adjusting to the loss of her eyesight. She spends hours in the chapel; there is always someone to take her on walks. She manages to work—baking bread, setting the table, washing dishes or answering the phone. Her farm column for the paper is so charming that it greatly increases the throng of our visitors to Staten Island. She continues her studies through "talking books" supplied by the public library, and is studying Braille.

Then there is Judith Gregory, who is away now, getting her master's degree in political science at the University of Virginia. When Judy is in the city working at St. Joseph's Hospitality House, she keeps her nose buried in desk work. She sits there answering the mail, sending out papers, and filling orders for books and pamphlets—and carrying on the most heated discussions on anything from politics to religion with any of the college crowd who happen to drop in.

Judy throws herself into everything she does with single-minded intensity. I noticed this the summer she spent on Staten Island, where she hadn't paperwork to deal with, but people. One young visitor was about to have a baby. Judy began devouring books on obstetrics in case we should get caught with no car on hand and no ambulance available from the hospital nearby. (This was no remote possibility; the beatnik girl with long black hair who had been staying with us several years before had her baby delivered by a policeman!) As it turned out, we were able to take the girl to a hospital. After the baby was born, Judy dedicated herself with equal fervor to its care, getting up all through the night to warm formulas and taking personal charge of the mother around the clock.

She also found time that summer to teach the illiterate to sing folk songs and rounds after supper, whether they had any voice for it or not. Judy's enthusiasm for nature in itself makes her a delight to be with. She collects ferns as I collect seaweed, with this difference: I collect without classifying, mainly for the joy of walking along the beach, but Judy knows the Latin name for every fern.

Among our editors is Anne Marie Taillefer, who does book reviews, poetry, and articles for the paper. She also gives out the women's garments at the house on Chrystie Street because she so loves clothes—even second-hand ones. Anne Marie lives in a small penthouse atop a hotel near Times Square. Not all penthouses in New York are elegant and spacious, nor is hers. But she has room enough to dispense hospitality and is always taking in some homeless person or other.

She spends a great deal of time at the United Nations, working with one of the nongovernmental agencies. She is often asked, "Whom do you represent?" Her only answer is "Myself." For days at a time she has kept in her home visitors from other lands, people of other races, many of whom speak no English. This has given rise to complicated situations, but she has always managed to surmount them somehow.

Bob Steed, who came to us after helping a house of hospitality in Memphis six years ago, made up the paper for some years. I am usually on hand to select the material, but Bob did the actual makeup. He now works twelve hours every night as attendant in a parking lot. (It's not that he loves work all that much. He's saving money for a trip to Paris.) Bob is another of our editors who served a prison sentence. After the Cuban invasion, he spent ten days in a Washington jail for picketing the CIA. Now Tom Cornell takes his place in getting out the paper.

Also working in the office these last years on the paper, and in the house of hospitality, have been: Philip Havey, not long back from his thirty-three days in prison as a Freedom Rider; Jim Forest, who was released from the Navy after he became a conscientious objector while in the service (both married this last year and left the work); Walter Kerrell, a convert, exercising his creative urge all over the place—writing poetry, painting each one of the file drawers a different color, or designing African masks on horseshoe crabs to place above the editors' desks; Ed Forand, ex-Marine, a good journalist, who gets up at four in the morning to beg a crate of vegetables from the market, and who drives the car and shares the cooking with Charles and Walter; Jean Morton, who helped in many ways, including picketing and peace marches, as did little Sharon Farmer, who married Phil Havey, the day she became eighteen; Dianne Gannon and Stuart Sanberg, both twenty-one, who started a new venture, the Siloem House for children, just around the corner. Dianne is now working and studying in a Montessori school, and Stuart is in a seminary in Washington.

Other members of the staff at this writing are Martin Corbin, who is married and has three children, earning his living at the Libertarian Press and living with the community at Glen Gardner, New Jersey; and Ed Turner, who walked out of the Army to become a conscientious objector and served two years in prison for his beliefs. Ed is married to my goddaughter, Johannah

Hughes, and he not only teaches and writes but is doing research on Peter Maurin and his teaching. Karl Meyer, who is head of the Chicago house of hospitality, is, at twenty-four, one of the best writers on the paper. Arthur Sheehan and his wife Elizabeth are long and much loved associates.

But there have been so many with us over the years who have come and become part of us and, though they have gone, left their mark. It would be impossible to remember them all, let alone make a list of them—for which the reader may be grateful!

In late afternoon, those waiting for dinner
at St. Joseph's House of Hospitality
pass the time reading the newspapers,
smoking, or visiting.

Part IV

Things
That Happen

< *Dorothy Day was sentenced to thirty days in*
the Women's House of Detention, in Greenwich Village,
for refusing to participate in civilian air raid drills.
In this picture she is being booked.

Chapter 13

What Has Become of Anna?

"WHAT HAS BECOME OF ANNA?" SOMEONE JUST ASKED. HOW, HOW to keep track over the years of those who come and go? All we can answer is that we believe she is staying in a home for the aged somewhere in New York.

Anna was a short, shuffling woman with a broad, flat face, a big, smiling mouth, and little tufts of hair growing out of her chin. She began visiting us when we lived on Mott Street. For a long while, she would only poke her nose in the door and ask for bread and coffee; she would not come into the house. When we moved to Chrystie Street Anna followed us with her brown cardboard carton that held all her belongings. She had attached a heavy cord to it so that she could drag it after her. Usually she wore several dresses and several coats. She peeled off the layers acording to the weather. Anna's vanity showed only in her style of headdress. She was always winding strange pieces of silk of many colors around her head in fantastic turbans. One time she appeared with her head wrapped in a bright peach-colored piece of woman's underwear. We gently persuaded her to dispense with this.

Anna was poor yet not destitute. She would never take an entire cigarette—that was too good for her, she said. She preferred to pick up butts. She loved her tobacco and coffee, and she was always cheerful. Her eyes twinkled, she smiled continually. Her two favorite topics of conversation were marriage and the benign spirits that surrounded her.

When she finally started to come in for meals, she would

leave right after supper. If anyone asked where she lived she was vague. She slept around, she told us: sometimes in a Jewish bakery, sometimes in a vacant store, sometimes in doorways.

We felt we had achieved a great victory when she consented to stay with us. "But I won't sleep in a bed," she said. "I haven't slept in one for thirty years. I can't begin now." So she took a corner of the hallway where no one passed. She would curl up there with a bundle under her head. One cold night I ventured to put a blanket over her. She got up hastily, left the house, and did not come back for several days. If we left a blanket lying around the office, however, she would pick it up and use it. She was our guest in this way for five years or more.

Three years ago, when we received our eviction notice from the city, we planned to move to the only available place we could find, the loft on Spring Street. We did not know what to do about Anna. We were permitted to use the loft as a day center but not as sleeping quarters. Besides, it was unheated. On Chrystie Street we always kept the heat up at night for her sake. We still had the few apartments we had rented in the old neighborhood, but Anna would not bunk with Scotch Mary, or Hatty, or any of the other women.

Then, shortly before we moved, someone picked up the *Daily News* one morning and read that Anna had been run down by a bus as she was crossing a street, dragging her carton after her. She was in Gouverneur Hospital with two broken legs and other injuries, and there she had to remain for almost a year. When the old people's home took her in she looked back with nostalgia to her old freedom, life on the streets, and her bed on our floor.

Before they settled her, the welfare workers were kind enough to bring her around in a cab so that she could see for herself how impossible it would be for her to return. She would have had to climb our stairs in her comings and goings.

Our aim is to make people happy. We certainly succeeded with Anna in the end, but it took years before she made herself at home with us. She exemplified the fantastic lengths to which a human being will go in order to hang on to freedom and privacy.

Chapter 14

The Bodenheims

EVERY DAY AT TWELVE-THIRTY A BELL CALLS US TO THE ROSARY in the reading room at Chrystie Street. Those who wish to, gather together to pray for peace in the world. Sometimes mothers and children who've come for clothes are caught waiting there. They share in prayer if they like, or they just sit. Slim goes on rocking, a cigar—if he has managed one—stuck in his mouth. But generally the attitude is one of reverent attention. Some sit upright, some kneel crouching over chairs in strange, grotesque positions.

Around eleven-thirty one day, Max Bodenheim, the poet who became a legendary symbol of the old Greenwich Village bohemia, came in with his wife, Ruth. It was the first time I had seen him in years. Max was dragging a broken leg in a cast. They told me they had been evicted from their furnished room; they needed shelter. Could they, Ruth asked, go to one of the farms? There happened to be room at Maryfarm, and Charlie could drive them up that same day.

So Max settled himself in the library, directly behind the table where the statue of the Blessed Mother stood, to wait for Ruth to bring their few belongings from a friend's house. He was caught there when the rosary started. Seeing him in back of the statue, the flowers, and the lighted candles distracted me. I could not help thinking, Poor Max, suddenly trapped like this, with dozens of other ragged, down-and-out people who come into the room at the ringing of a bell, planting themselves all around him and praying. He must feel besieged, as if they are praying for him, or at him. When the prayer was over, I went outside to the hall and saw Ruth sitting on her suitcase, reading some of Max's poems which she was sorting out of another broken suitcase by her side. She was a picture of the abandoned. I apologized. "We're not forcing prayers on anyone," I told her. "It's just that it's the only place we have to pray."

"Max is a Catholic," she said, smiling. "Baptized, made his first Communion, and confirmed, too, down in Mississippi, where he was born. His mother was from Alsace-Lorraine." Later I found out that she herself was baptized. According to her story, one of her parents was Catholic—probably her father, since her name was Fagan. Ruth was a Libertarian Socialist. She attended the meetings of that group, and carried pamphlets about the labor movement around with her.

Max and Ruth stayed at Maryfarm for a month or six weeks. She began making eyes at a Russian guest, who kissed her hand and flirted outrageously with her while he crudely insulted her husband. When Max began threatening the Russian with his cane I took the Bodenheims to Peter Maurin Farm, on Staten Island.

It was a bitter day; Ruth had a touch of the flu and didn't want to leave. She had been enjoying her flirtation. She was thirty-five; Max was sixty-five. A beautiful woman, with strong Jewish features, a splendid figure, and a great warmth of manner, she could have played a Judith or an Esther.

Max occasionally came to Mass, but Ruth never came. She told me she believed only in love. Yet I feel she was in love with herself in particular, with her own beauty, which she used to inflame men. Nevertheless, she certainly loved Max, and with compassion. She had met him on a New York street one rainy night two years before. He was in such forlorn condition that she took him home with her, and they were married not long afterward. (Max had been divorced by his first wife, Minna. He had a son he hadn't seen in eight years.)

I had known Max in the old days in Greenwich Village. When Gene O'Neill used to recite "The Hound of Heaven" to me in the back room of an old saloon on Fourth Street, Max was there, one of the habitués. He sat at a table, writing poetry on the backs of old envelopes. I remember one long poem that he and Gene and I wrote together, each doing a verse in turn. Max didn't drink much then; he was a hard worker. He was beginning to turn out novels and books of poetry, but none of them sold very well. He tried to get money by giving poetry readings. He had already lost most of his front teeth, and between his lisp, his stammer, and his pipe, it was hard to understand him. Despite the picture the newspapers drew of him as a Don Juan, he was never a very prepossessing person.

Max and Ruth remained with us at Peter Maurin Farm until after Easter. On Easter Sunday Max went to Mass. Ruth went into town regularly, trying to peddle some of Max's poetry in hope of getting a room again. Finally she sold one poem to the *New York Times*. It didn't bring them much, but they rejoiced for weeks.

When she was away Max would not eat. Every now and then, after a long silence, he would ask me, "Do you think my beloved wife will be back this evening?" He hardly talked at all, but every day or so he produced another poem. He lay on one of the two beds we had set up in the shape of an L in a warm hall bedroom and rested, meditated, smoked his pipe, and wrote.

Spring came, bringing warm weather. Now his leg was out of the cast. One day, without a word, Max and Ruth disappeared. After a few days, she came back to get some things she had left in a seaman's duffel bag. She and her companion, a young man, rather somber and silent, picked it up and walked down the road to the train late that night.

I never saw Ruth or Max again. The next year they were murdered in the Third Avenue room of a young fellow who had given them shelter. Max was shot and Ruth was beaten and stabbed. Three days later the police caught this demented friend, Weinberg, as he was seeking a place to sleep in the basement of a rooming house on Twenty-first Street.

I read the account of this brutal slaying in all the papers on February 8. They were ugly stories, portraying all the worst of Max and Ruth. Max was presented as a drunken bohemian, a clown, an exhibitionist, a lecher; Ruth, as a woman loose in morals, depraved in appetite, who loved Max only for his prestige as a writer and poet and found her sexual satisfaction with casual young men. Only a few papers gave him some credit for achievement, noting that he had won literary awards and that he was the author of fourteen novels as well as several books of poetry. In spite of all this hard work, his life had been spent in dire poverty.

Ruth once told me he had been married a second time to an invalid, on whom he had lavished what care he could afford from the sale of the reprint rights to his books when they came out in paperback editions. To get the few hundred dollars to pay for food and medicines and doctors, and later for her burial, he had sacrificed all claim to other royalties.

Max was buried in a family plot in New Jersey. A rabbi officiated at his funeral, the expenses of which were paid by the poet Alfred Kreymbourg, some say (others say Ben Hecht). Many friends came to his funeral and many followed him to his grave. There was no possibility of a Catholic burial, since he had not practiced his faith since childhood.

We had been able to do little for Max or Ruth. The bare bones of hospitality we gave them. If we had loved them more, if Ruth had found more love with us, perhaps she would not have wandered around searching pathetically for the only kind of warmth and light and color she knew in the ugly gray life around her. We were able to do so little; God must listen to our prayers for them.

And poor Weinberg. A homeless child, placed in a Hebrew orphanage at an early age, put into a mental hospital when he was ten and never once visited by his mother, released at the age of seventeen only to go into the Army, serve for seven months, and then be discharged as unfit for service. Shut off from life and from people, without faith, without hope, without love, he earned his miserable meals by miserable work—dishwashing, the one job open to the unskilled, the unorganized, the mentally or physically crippled. He took the only kind of love he knew, bodily love, wherever he could find it—in this case from a woman as mentally clouded as himself—and he expressed his anger bodily, too.

There was also violence in Ruth. She wanted men to fight over her. It seems instinctual to many women to want to be so desired that men will pay any price for their favors. And where there is no money, blood will often do.

When arraigned, Max's murderer cried out, "I have killed two Communists. I should get a medal!" There was malice in the smile he turned on the police and the reporters.

Max was a poet; he was sympathetic to the Communists because they spoke in terms of bread and shelter, and he had long lived with hunger. Drink became his refuge. (Drink is often easier to get than bread.) When he was young he wrote free verse, but in those last years, when he was the most disorganized, his verse became formal and stylized. Every day he was with us he worked on a series of sonnets, each dedicated to one of us. They were courteous, stately, polished, though often obscure; he came to meals happily to read them aloud for our applause. I especially remember one he wrote to our Agnes, the widow of a barge captain. I loved this delicate appreciation of her sweetness and diligence, her care for our comfort.

Agnes had charge of the second-floor bedrooms, the linens and the bathroom. Never once did she criticize or complain about the wild disorder that accompanied such guests as Max and Ruth. No matter how comfortable, how tidy a room was when they entered it, it soom became a shambles of dirty socks, rags, scuffed shoes, dust, cigarette butts, newspapers, onions, bread, apple cores, empty coffee cups, paper bags.

The newspapers emphasized the sordidness of the room on Third Avenue where their bodies were found. As I read, I thought how, over and over again, I have seen just such rooms in our houses of hospitality. They reflect the grim and hopeless chaos of the minds of their occupants, the disorder of people who do not appreciate the material even while seeking in it all their pleasures.

In trying to save the life of the flesh, the Bodenheims were most hideously tricked. May their poor, dark, tormented souls be at rest.

Chapter 15

Strange Visitors, Distinguished Visitors

ONE DAY A TALL, GOOD-LOOKING, WELL-DRESSED MAN WALKED IN with a black snake coiled around his neck. Ammon Hennacy, who is fearless and refuses to be surprised by anything, took the snake, caressed it, and then advised the man to take it away. There had been a few shrieks from the women. With only one exit from the loft, aside from the fire escape, we always dreaded the danger of a panic.

Jim—that was our visitor's name—took the snake away, but the next day he came in with a young boa constrictor twined around his arm. "You could not wear this one around your neck," he explained. "It would choke you for sure." We have persuaded him not to bring snakes into the office. I've heard that the black snake has died and that he is going to have it stuffed for me. I wonder if, when I go to the office someday, I will not see it curled up on my desk as a present. Jim has machetes, shillelaghs a hooked knife of a kind used to castrate steers, bear traps, apple-peeling machines, and other choice decorations which he has brought to the office and hung around the walls. The knife hangs suspended by a cord over one of the desks.

"Why are there so many mad people around The Catholic Worker?" Jim asked one day, with a sigh. Last week, when he came in after an absence of a year, I asked him what pets he had now, and out of his pocket he pulled a large snail!

We have another friend, a Russian writer and doctor, with wrinkles around his smiling lips and a perpetual inquiry in his eyes. "Why don't you serve the breadline with wine instead of coffee?" Basil used to ask me. "It would be much better for them and not so expensive." I agreed that, in general, wine maketh glad the heart of man, and that a little would be good for the stomach's sake. "Why don't you do it yourself?" I asked him finally. "If you think they should be served wine, why not get some and serve it?"

Easter was approaching, so he agreed that he would come at noon, when we served the traditional Easter feast of ham, applesauce, sweet potatoes, and pie. I forgot about his proposal; I had not really taken it seriously. But on Easter Day Basil arrived in a taxi and with the driver's help began carrying out the wine. He brought with him twenty gallons in all, and a carton of paper cups. Ceremonially, with great courtesy, he served everyone, putting a cup of wine at each place. Breadlines are usually solemn and wordless affairs. Men eat what is put

The unofficial doorman at Chrystie Street asks people who are too noisy to leave—but never has the heart to stick by his order and always lets them back a few minutes later with grave warnings. A note on the window reads, "No men's clothes today."

in front of them and go out quickly so that those who are waiting can be served. If they see there is plenty, or if they notice another great pot of steaming soup on the back of the stove, they go to the end of the line and come back to be served again.

But, when the wine was set in front of them that day, their eyes lit up: a grateful, happy, and amused look spread over their faces. A few gallons of wine were left over for supper for the house (we numbered another hundred). Those who were too susceptible abstained (Alcoholics Anonymous holds meetings with us), but those who could take it, took it.

"What are you trying to do, wreck the place?" a social worker who was helping us asked me angrily. "Have you gone mad?"

When Basil left, he was quiet and happy. He said only, "You should have had paper napkins."

Once, when I was visiting in West Virginia, where my daughter was living at the time, I received a telegram from *Life* magazine: "Will you have lunch with Evelyn Waugh? He wishes to meet American writers."

I was thirty-five miles from the nearest town of any size, twelve miles from the village, and two miles from the crossroads store. Also, the car had broken down. I did not answer the telegram, thinking I could telephone when I returned to New York in a few days. When I got back a second telegram came, then a telephone call, each changing the date and place of the appointment. A final telegram was a request to meet Mr. Waugh at the Chambord Restaurant at one o'clock on Wednesday. Jack English laughed heartily at this. "The Chambord! It's one of the most expensive restaurants in town," he said. "People like the Duke and Duchess of Windsor eat there. The place is famous for its wines. If you go there *Life* might very well carry a picture of the breadline next to one of you and Evelyn Waugh feasting, with the caption 'No soup for her.'"

We would impute no such malice to *Life* magazine, but Jack's devilish imagination had painted a picture that caused me concern. Out of politeness I telegraphed hastily: "Forgive my class consciousness but the Chambord appalls me as Mott Street does you."

This evoked an immediate response from Mr. Waugh, who telephoned personally. He would meet me anywhere I suggested. So he came first to Mott Street, and then we went on to an Italian restaurant on Mulberry Street, where I am afraid the prices were way too high and the food not too good. But Mr. Waugh was kind. "It's the austerity regime in England," he explained. "I just wanted a good meal, which was why I suggested the Chambord." I think that he wanted to treat us to a good meal, too, for he also took Jack and Tom Sullivan and Bob Ludlow and Irene Naughton. I remember Tom arguing with him over poverty in a vine-clad cottage in Ireland and the falling birthrate there, and the misery of the rich, and all of us debating whether the poor or the rich had the worst of it in this world.

Since then he sends us checks every now and then, always made out to "Dorothy Day's Soup Kitchen." He does not recognize the anarchist-pacifist Catholic Worker as anything other than a movement that has to do with feeding people. And perhaps he is right. Food and the land, and the work which coordinates them, are indeed fundamental.

And there was the night in the forties, when Michael Grace, two members of the Kennedy family, and some others came to visit us at Mott Street. Because it is more comfortable to argue over food and drink, we all went over to the Muni, not the municipal shelter but an all-night restaurant on Canal Street, where they serve cheese blintzes and chav and borscht. We had coffee and cheesecake and talked until the small hours. I remember only that we talked of war and peace and of man and the state. I do not remember which of the Kennedy boys were there, but those who do remember tell me it was our President, John Kennedy, and his older brother Joseph, who lost his life in the war.

Chapter 16

The "Cold Turkey" Cure

FOR YEARS WE AT THE CATHOLIC WORKER PERFORMED ALL THE works of mercy except visiting the prisoner. We had tried to accomplish the equivalent of this through working for the release of political prisoners and speaking in their behalf. We had a chance to practice this act of love in another way in recent years, when we made our stand against the yearly war game of taking shelter during the air-raid drill by refusing to comply with the law. We visited prisoners by becoming prisoners ourselves for five years running, until the Civil Defense authorities dropped the compulsory drills.

It was Ammon Hennacy's idea to go out into the city parks to distribute literature calling attention to the penance we need to do as the first nation to use nuclear weapons at Hiroshima and Nagasaki. Pointing out on good authority that there could be no shelter against nuclear attacks, he always dwelt on the duty of civil disobedience in order to call attention to the hideous dangers hanging over the world today, and our personal responsibility to do something about them.

It was not a question of obedience to the law or to duly constituted authority. Law must be according to right reason, and the law that made it compulsory to take shelter was a mockery. In our disobedience we were trying to obey God rather than men, trying to follow a higher obedience. We did not wish to act in a spirit of defiance and rebellion. Ours was a small matter compared to the problem confronting the German, for instance, when he was called upon to obey Hitler. We were free to make our witness, and our jail sentences were light—five days on one occasion, thirty days on another, and fifteen days the last time. Fellow pacifists have spent months in jail since then— some for protesting the building of a missile base, some, the launching of nuclear submarines; others served many months in a prison in Hawaii for illegally sailing into the Pacific testing area.

We were setting our faces against things as they are, against the terrible injustice our basic capitalist industrial system per- petrates by making profits out of preparations for war. But espec- ially we wanted to act against war and getting ready for war: nerve gas, germ warfare, guided missiles, testing and stockpiling of nuclear bombs, conscription, the collection of income tax— against the entire militarism of the state. We made our gesture; we disobeyed a law. The law we broke was the Civil Defense Act, one provision of which stipulated that everyone must take shelter for ten minutes during a sham air raid. We always gave the Civil Defense authorities, the police, and the press notice of what we intended to do. Among us in 1957, for instance, were Ammon Hennacy, Kerran Dugan and Deane Mowrer from The Catholic Worker. Judith and Julian Beck, heads of the Living Theatre group, called up the night before to say they were joining us. Judith had begun by distributing leaflets with us two years before and had been arrested with us then. We were held in jail overnight and later given suspended sentences. The second year we had served five-day sentences. This year the group included five Catholics, two Jews, two Protestants, and three who were of no faith. Richard and Joan Moses of the Fellowship of Reconcilation picketed independently in Times Square, thinking that ours was a Catholic demonstration; they received the same sentence. We truly represented a pluralist society. We regretted only that there were no Negroes among us.

At the Women's House of Detention, where we were held, five doctors are in attendance, also nurses and nurses's aides. First, preliminary tests and examinations, X-rays, cardiographs, blood tests, smears, and so on are taken. Every morning for the duration of one's stay, the shout "Clinic!" reverberates through the corridors. Girls leave their workshops or their cells to vary the monotony of their days by waiting in line for an aspirin, heat rash lotion, gargle, eyewash, or other innocuous remedies. In addition they have the refreshment of a visit with inmates from other floors.

Play is encouraged: bingo, basketball, interpretive dancing, and calisthenics—but sexual play is the most popular and is indulged in openly every evening on the roof, when the girls put on rock 'n' roll records. Living two to a cell does not help matters; yet the authorities have denied any overcrowding, ever since a new ruling was passed granting ten days off a month for good behavior for the long-term women. Just before we pacifists came in to serve our thirty-day sentence, a great many prisoners were released on this basis. All the same, most cells on our floor held two cots, which made our six-by-nine rooms more crowded than the tiniest hall bedroom.

One stout woman with a cell to herself was so cramped on the very narrow cot on which she was supposed to sleep that she hitched it up against the wall by its iron chain, spread a blanket out on the cement floor, and slept there.

We four political prisoners had cells next to each other. We were two in a cell, on the most airless corridor, with the darkest cubicles. We had a dim, twenty-five-watt bulb in ours, Judith Beck and I, until the last week of our thirty days, when a tall young colored woman brought us a fifty-watt bulb from a neighboring cell just vacated. Our windows faced north and look out over the old Jefferson Market court. We felt that we had been put there because the picketing meant to call attention to our imprisonment was going on along the south side of the jail. From the other corridors we might have seen the line. Our windows were small, and there was no cross-ventilation. Opposite us the showers steamed with heat. One of the captains said she thought that by putting us in this "good" corridor, next to each other, she was doing us a favor; but it was so obviously the least desirable, the most airless and dark, that I do not see how she could honestly have thought that. Perhaps she did. I do know that, from the time one is arrested until the time one leaves a prison, every event seems calculated to intimidate and to render uncomfortable and ugly the life of the prisoner.

I couldn't help thinking how entirely opposite is the work of the Good Shepherd nuns, who care for delinquent girls after they have been sentenced by the state. Their Mother Foundress said that her aim was to make the girls happy, comfortable, and industrious; she surrounded her charges with love and devotion, and with the expectation of good.

"Here we are treated like animals," one girl said to me, "so why shouldn't we act like animals?" Animals, however, are not capable of the unmentionable verbal filth that punctuates the conversation of prisoners. So these prisoners are, in a way, pushed below the animal level. I can only hint at the daily, hourly repetitive obscenity that pervades a prison. Shouts, jeers, defiance of guards and each other, expressed in these ways, reverberated through the cells and corridors even at night, while, gripping my rosary, I tried to pray. Noise—that is perhaps the greatest torture in jail. It stings the ear and stuns the mind. After I came out it took me at least a week to recover from it. The city itself seemed silent. Down the corridor from me was a strong, healthy Polish woman who should have used her great vitality rearing children instead of dissipating it in prostitution and drugs. She often held her head in her hands and cried. Even to her the noise was torture. Yet she herself, almost without knowing it, was one of the worst offenders. When she started screeching her ribald stories at night, her voice reverberated from cell to cell. "But this place was not made to live in," she said, pointing to the iron bars, the cement, and the walls. "The ceilings are low, the sounds bounce around."

Everything *was* exaggeratedly loud. Television blared from the "rec" room on each floor in the most distorted way. One heard not words or music, only clamor. The clanging of gates—seventy gates on a floor—the pulling of the master lever, which locked all the cells in each corridor at one stroke, the noise of the three elevators, the banging of pots and pans and dishes from the dining room, all these made the most unimaginable din, not to mention the shoutings of human voices.

The guard (there is one to a floor) has to have strong lungs to make herself heard; ours was one who could. She looked like a stern schoolteacher; she seldom smiled and never "fraternized." The women respected her; "She's an honest cop," one of them said of her. "She's just what she is and does not pretend to be anything else." That meant that she did not become friendly with the girls—neither honestly trying to help them nor becoming overly familiar.

I saw a few of the guards being treated with the greatest effrontery by the prisoners, who kidded them and even whacked them across the behind as they went in and out of the elevator. Much of this was greeted by the guards with smiling tolerance.

On the other hand, a "good" officer had to know just how far to go in severity, too: just how firm to be and just how much to put up with, to overlook. I saw one guard trying to hasten a prisoner's exit from the auditorium, where the inmates had just put on a show, with what we took to be a friendly push. The prisoner turned on her viciously, threateningly. On such occasions the officers do not press the point. They realize they are sitting on a volcano. They know when to back down. But a number of times, witnessing their humiliation, I was ashamed for them. The hostility of the Negro for the white often flares up then. Helpless as the prisoner may seem to be, she knows, too, that she has the superior numbers on her side, that she can start something if she wants to and maybe get away with it. She is also aware of the worst she can expect. In many cases the worst has already happened to her: she has undergone the "cold turkey" treatment.

While in prison I received a letter inviting me to speak on television. It had already been opened by the censor and commented on all over the House of Detention. The girls came to me and begged me to plead their case to the world: "You must tell how we are put here for long terms, and about the cold turkey cure, too; about how we are thrown in 'the tank' and left

164

to lie there in our own vomit and filth, too sick to move, too sick even to get to the open toilet in the cell."

One girl added, "I had to clean out those cells." They are called tanks because they are kept bare of furnishings and can be hosed out, I suppose. The "cooler," on the other hand, is the punishment cell; there are several of them on various floors. Here a recalcitrant prisoner is kept in solitary for brief periods, until she "cools off."

I heard stories of padded cells; of cells with only ventilating systems but no window, no open bars, in which a girl sits in the dark; of cells where water can be turned on in some kind of sprinkler system to assist the process of cooling off. I heard of girls being thrown naked into these cells on the pretext that they might use some article of clothing to make a rope to hang themselves. I heard of girls breaking the crockery bowls and using the shards to try to cut their throats or their wrists. I heard of girls who had tried to hang themselves by their belts. But I know none of these things of my own knowledge. From the open elevator door, as we journeyed to and from clinic or workshop, I saw only the gruesome steel-plated doors, ominous indicators of the presence of these punishment cells.

Most cells for the five hundred or so prisoners, or girls held in "detention," are cemented and tiled halfway up the front, and then barred to the ceiling; about ten bars across the front of the cell, perhaps five bars to the gate, which is so heavy one can hardly move it. It is the crowning indignity for the officers to shout, "Close your gates!" and to have to shut oneself in. The open bars at the top enable one to call the guard, to call out to other prisoners, to carry on some friendly intercourse. The "cooler" is meant to be a place of more severe punishment than the cell, so it is completely closed in.

"*Tell how we are treated!*" they cried to me. I can only tell the things that I have seen with my eyes, heard with my ears. The reports of the other prisoners will not be considered credible. After all, they are prisoners; why should they be believed? People will say, "What! Do you believe self-confessed thieves, prostitutes, drug addicts, criminals who are in jail for assault, for putting out the eyes of others, for stabbing, and other acts of violence?"

Perhaps it is a little too much to believe that twenty girls have died in the House of Detention from the cold turkey cure these last two years, as one inmate charged. But there have been grim stories which appeared in the *New York Times*, and in other New York papers. I heard one young addict tell the story of a girl who died in the cell, after her "cellie," as the roommate is called, had cried out over and over again for the officer to come and administer to the sick girl. When the doctor finally came, hours later, after the cells were unlocked, she was dead. Two prisoners assaulted the doctor and kept her head poked down the open toilet while another prisoner kept flushing it in an attempt to drown her. "Her head shook from that time on, as though she had palsy," one of the other girls said, with grim satisfaction.

I repeat, these are tales I heard told and repeated. They may be legends, but legends have a kernel of truth.

Ill treatment? How intangible a thing it sometimes is to report! Whenever I was asked by the officers and captains and the warden himself how I was making out, how I was being treated, I could only say that everything was all right so far as I was concerned. After all, I was only in for twenty-five days, what with the five days off for good behavior. I had no complaint to make against individuals, and yet one must complain about everything—the atmosphere, the attitude, the ugliness of it all. "After all, we don't want to make this place glamorous," the guards protested. How many times when a prisoner was released I heard them say, "You'll be back!" as if to set a stamp of hopelessness on any effort the prisoner might make to reform.

Listening to the prisoners talk about the kick they got out of drugs, I saw how impossible it was for them to conceive of themselves as "squares" (people who go to work every day) and how hopelessly they regarded the world outside, which they nevertheless longed for hourly. They made me feel, too, that without a "community"—in the early Christian sense—to return to, their future was indeed bleak.

But, I wondered, must the attempt to keep the place "unglamorous" cause so many small indignities to be heaped on each prisoner? Why cannot they be treated as they are in the Good Shepherd Homes (where they are sentenced for two years or more), as children of God, and made happy and comfortable? The very deprivation of freedom is sufficient punishment. For the prisoners the breaking of vicious habits is difficult enough.

I have received letters from *Catholic Worker* readers who have been prison officers and officials which showed the same lack of understanding, and I could only think, What if *they* were treated as prisoners? What if they were crowded into a bullpen, a metal cage, awaiting trial, then transported in a sealed van with no springs where they are tossed from seat to ceiling in real danger of broken bones and bruised spines; or stripped naked, lined up, and prodded rudely, even roughly, in the search for drugs; or dressed in inadequate garments coming only to the knees, and then, with every belonging from rosary to prayer book to Testament taken away, led off to a permanent cell and there locked behind bars? Envisaging our critics, our chaplains, our catechists under such circumstances, seeing *them* shivering nakedly, obeying blindly, pushed hither and yon, I could not help but think that it is only by experiencing such things that one can understand and have compassion for one's brother.

Yet many priests and nuns around the world have had these experiences in Russia, Germany, and Japan in our generation. In the face of the suffering of our time one is glad to go to prison, if only to share these sufferings.

Our friends and readers will remind us of the beatings, the torture, the brainwashings in the prisons of Russia and Germany. As for beatings, third-degree methods are generally accepted in our own land. I have read of them, heard of them from parole officers as well as from prisoners. In the case of sex offenders and offenders against little children, brutality is repaid with brutality. One prisoner, a drug addict, told me that she had been so beaten by members of the narcotics squad trying to make her tell where she had gotten her drugs that they were unable to arrest her for fear they themselves would be held criminally liable for her condition—which goes to show that if beating is not accepted in theory it is nonetheless practiced.

Some time ago the magazine section of the *New York Times* carried a long article on the treatment of drug addicts in Great Britain. There they are regarded not as criminals but as patients and are so treated, through clinics and custodial care. Here they are made into criminals by our "control" methods, which make the drug so hard to get that the addict turns to crime to get it. Many criminologists believe that we should reform our thinking in this regard. At a recent meeting one prison official said that nowadays a prison term is a life sentence on the installment plan. And so it is with drug addicts. The girl who told of the beating and other ill treatment had started to use drugs when she was twelve and became a prostitute at that time. She had been in prison sixteen times since and was now twenty-two.

As for the problem of prostitution, most of the girls openly admitted it. "I'm a pross," they would tell us. "I was money hungry." Or "I wanted a car," or "I wanted drugs." They felt the injustice of the woman being arrested and not the man. They despised the tactics of the plain-clothesmen who solicited them to trap them. The grossest misconception held not only by prostitutes but also by some pious people is that were it not for the prostitute there would be far more sex crimes. I heard this statement made by Matilda, a girl down the corridor, one evening when she was in an unusually quiet and philosophical mood. Matilda pointed out that, in their demands on prostitutes, jaded men want to explore every perversion, to the disgust of what society considers the lowest of women, whores and dope fiends. These are not pretty words nor are they pretty thoughts. But everything comes out into the open in jail. "The more I see of men," one girl said, "the more I'd prefer relations with a woman." And another pretty girl added wistfully, "I've got to get used to the idea of men, so that I can have a baby."

Cardinal Newman once wrote that not even to save the world (or to save good women and little children) could a single venial sin be committed. When I lay in jail thinking of these things, thinking of war and peace and the problem of human freedom, of jails, drug addiction, prostitution, and the apathy of great masses of people who believe that nothing can be done—when I thought of these things I was all the more confirmed in my faith in the little way of St. Thérèse. We do the things that come to hand, we pray our prayers and beg also for an increase of faith—and God will do the rest.

One of the greatest evils of the day among those outside of prison is their sense of futility. Young people say, What good can one person do? What is the sense of our small effort? They cannot see that we must lay one brick at a time, take one step at a time; we can be responsible only for the one action of the present moment. But we can beg for an increase of love in our hearts that will vitalize and transform all our individual actions, and know that God will take them and multiply them, as Jesus multiplied the loaves and fishes.

Next year, perhaps, God willing, we will go again to jail; and conditions will perhaps be the same. To be charitable, we can only say that the prison officials do the best they can according to their understanding. In a public institution they are not paid to love the inmates; they are paid to guard them. They admit that the quarters are totally inadequate, that what was built as a house of detention for women awaiting trial is now being used as a workhouse and penitentiary.

When the girls asked me to speak for them, to tell the world outside about "conditions," they emphasized the crowded and confined surroundings. "We are here for years—to work out our sentences, not just for detention!" Shut in by walls, bars, concrete, and heavy iron screenings so that even from the roof one's vision of the sky is impeded, mind and body suffer from the strain. Nerves clamor for change, for open air, more freedom of movement.

The men imprisoned over on Hart Island and Riker's Island can get out and play ball, can work on the farm or in the tree nursery. They can see all around them—water and boats and seagulls—and breathe the sea air coming from the Atlantic. The women have long been promised North Brother Island as a

*Dorothy Day, under arrest for refusal to participate
in a civil defense drill, was taken
to the Women's House of Detention.*

companion institution. But that island is being used to confine teen-age addicts. And there are other seemingly insuperable obstacles in the way. Money figures largely. There is money for civil defense drills, for death rather than for life, money for all sorts of nonsensical expenditures, but none for these least of God's children suffering in the midst of millions of people who are scarcely aware of their existence. "Nothing short of a riot will change things," one warden told us. Was he perhaps suggesting that we pacifists start one?

If those who read this will pray for the prisoners—if New York readers, when they pass the Women's House of Detention, will look up, perhaps wave a greeting, say a prayer, there will be the beginning of a change. Two of the women, Tulsa and Thelma, said that they never looked out through those bars; they could not stand it. But most of the other prisoners do, and perhaps they will see this gesture; perhaps they will feel the caress of this prayer, and a sad heart will be lightened, and a resolution strengthened, and there will be a turning away from evil and toward the good. Christ is with us today, not only in the Blessed Sacrament, and where two or three are gathered together in His Name, but also in the poor. And who could be poorer or more destitute in body and soul than these companions of our twenty-five days in prison?

One of the peculiar enjoyments I got out of jail was in being on the other side for a change. Working in a laundry, for instance; ironing, mending the uniforms of jailers. For so many years I had been in charge of work, had been the adminstrator! It is too easy to forget that all we give is given to us to give. Nothing is ours. All we have to give is our time and patience, our love. How often we have failed in love, how often we have been brusque, cold, and indifferent: "Roger takes care of the clothes; you'll have to come back at ten o'clock." Or "Just sit in the library and wait." "Wait your turn; I'm busy." So it often goes.

But in jail it was I who was getting pushed about. I was told what I could or could not do, hemmed in by rules and regulations and red tape and bureaucracy. It made me see my faults, but it also made me see how much more we accomplish at The Catholic Worker by not asking questions or doing any investigating but by cultivating a spirit of trust. The whole jail experience was good for my soul. I realized again how much ordinary kindness can do. Graciousness is an old-fashioned word but it has a beautiful religious tradition. "Grace is participation in the divine life," according to the Church's teaching. "You'll be back!"—the common farewell to the prisoner—was, in effect, wishing them not to fare well. There was no "Goodbye—God be with you"—because there was not enough faith or hope or charity to conceive of a forgiving and loving God being with anyone so lost in vice and crime as prostitutes, drug addicts, and other criminals are supposed to be.

One great indignity is the examination given all women for possession of drugs. There is certainly no recognition given to the fact of political imprisonment. All of us were stripped and searched in the crudest way—even to the tearing of membranes so that bleeding resulted. Then there is the matter of clothes—the scanty garments, the so-called "wrappers," which scarcely wrap around one, the floppy cloth slippers which are impossible to keep on! In Russia, in Germany, and even in our own country, to strip the prisoner, to humiliate him, is a definite part and purpose of a jail experience. Even in the Army, making a man stand naked before his examiners is to treat him like a dumb beast or a slave.

Had it not been for our fellow prisoners, neither Deane nor I would have been able to get to Mass that first Sunday, since we had only wrappers to wear the first two days. The guards did not care and made no move to help us. Too much red tape to cut through, too much bureaucracy. They would not have thought of depriving us of food for ten days; if we had gone on a hunger strike, they would have been greatly worried. But they were indifferent to the loss we suffered at being deprived of food for our souls, which was more necessary at this point than food for the body. It was our fellow prisoners who recognized our need and got clothes together for us. From their own scanty stock they brought dresses, socks, shoes, underwear, so that we were enabled to leave the floor and get to Mass.

A great courtesy accorded us was a visit from the warden himself. Nothing like that had ever happened before, one of the girls assured us. He wanted to know about our demonstrations, why we had done it. He was a Hungarian Catholic, so perhaps it was easy to understand his confusion about our pacifism. What man who is a man, he thought, does not wish to resist a foreign aggressor, to defend his home and family? But the problem of the means to an end had never occurred to him. Nowadays it is pretty generally accepted that the end justifies the means. To his mind, one just could not be a pacifist today. It was an "impossible" position.

As to our attitude toward the prison and the prisoners, he could not understand our love for them, our not judging them. The idea of hating the sin and loving the sinner seemed beyond him. To him we seemed to be denying the reality of evil because we were upholding the prisoner. The evil was there, all right, frank and unabashed. It was inside and also outside the jail. But he did not know what we meant when we spoke of finding Christ in our prison companions.

His visit gave us our chance to complain. We complained about food wasted, poured out in ashcans—bread, stew, powdered milk, cereal, even huge containers of marmalade and jam. Meals are often good, especially on Sunday. If the girls and women had a penitentiary on North Brother Island or in some other rural spot, where they could raise their own food, or help provide it; if they could bake their own bread, milk cows, tend chickens, engage in healthy and creative activity, share in the responsibility of the institution, it could become a far better place; it could become, in its way, a community. I read of an experiment in the Suffolk County Jail, where the men are farming (some of them) at Yaphank; and not only the jail but the county home for the aged receives vegetables and milk from the farm without charge. They call it a "mutual aid program." A place out of the city would provide more room for shops, for school, and for recreation.

When we first went in, Judith used to say ardently, "When the peaceable revolution comes we will abolish all prisons, throw wide all doors." Several young prostitutes asked her when this would be. "Do you mean there is no need for prisons?" Certainly beginnings can be made, here and now; even the most powerless, humblest officer or attendant can begin—not by the drastic act of resigning, as Ammon Hennacy might suggest, but by each man's being good and kind himself and spreading that atmosphere wherever he is. The "means to the end" begins with each one of us.

I spoke earlier of how often I have failed in love. When we were locked that first night in a narrow cell, meant for one but holding two cots, we had just passed through an experience which was as ugly and horrifying as any I have ever undergone. We had been processed; as we got off the elevators on the seventh floor to be assigned to our cells, clutching our wrappers around us, we were surrounded by a group of young women, colored and white, who first surveyed us boldly and then started making ribald comments. Deane Mowrer and I are older women, though Deane is younger than I, and Judith Malina Beck is young and beautiful. She is an actress, which means that she carries herself consciously, alert to the gaze of others, responding to it. That night, her black hair hung down around her shoulders and her face was very pale, but she had managed to get some lipstick on before the officers took all her things away from her.

Immediately some of the women began to put on an act, quarreling among themselves. They surrounded us and the officer (herself young and pretty) who sat at the table in the main corridor. Shockingly enough, she, too, seemed to enter into the spirit of banter among the girls.

"Put her in my cell," one of the roughest of the Puerto Rican girls shouted, clutching at Judith. "Let me have her," another one called out. It was a real hubbub, distracting and sordid, and it came after hours spent with prison officials, officers, nurses, and so on.

I had a great sinking of the heart, a great sense of terror for Judith. Was this what jail meant? I had heard from Dave Dellinger how conscientious objectors were put to work with the roughest of prisoners, with a virtual invitation on the part of prison officials for the "patriotic-minded" to give them a working over. But we had not expected this type of assault. With the idea of protecting Judith, I *demanded*—and I used that term, too, just this once during my imprisonment—that she be put in my cell or Deane's, even if we had to be doubled up because of crowding. "I will make complaints," I said very firmly, "if you do not do this."

The jeering and controversy continued, but the officer stopped laughing and took us to our respective cells, putting Judith and me in one and Deane in another.

We felt a great sense of separation from the other prisoners, and as we were locked in that first night I thought of a recent story by Salinger I had read in *The New Yorker*. It is about the impact of the Prayer of Jesus, a famous prayer among pilgrims in Russia, on a young girl from an actor's family. The prayer, repeated hundreds of times, is, "My Lord Jesus Christ, Son of the Living God, have mercy on me a sinner." Sometimes the prayer is shortened: "My Lord Jesus, have mercy on me a sinner."

Frannie, the girl in Salinger's story, is in such a state over this prayer, repeating it ceaselessly, that her mother is about to get the advice of a psychiatrist. But the brother, who, with his sister, has been educated by an older brother who is something of a mystic, accomplishes his sister's release from her compulsion in a long conversation which makes the tale more a novelette than a short story. He finally convinces her that she is looking for a short cut to religious experience, that fundamentally she scorns other people and is turning to God to escape contact with humankind. He reminds her of a piece of advice given by the older brother. Acting in a radio play, she is to remember the fat lady sitting on her porch rocking and listening to the radio. In other words, "Jesus Christ is the fat lady," and she is to act with all her heart and love directed to the fat lady. Part of the impact of the story is the contrast between the reverence of the prayer and crude truth. The language—including a compulsive use of the name of God—is often shocking. But the profound Christian truth the story expresses has been repeated over and over again by the saints. In the words of Jesus to Catherine of Siena: "I have placed you in the midst of your fellows that you may do to them what you cannot do to Me, that is to say . . . that you may love your neighbors without expecting any return from them, and what you do to them I count as done to Me."

We were locked in our cells, and all the other five hundred women in the House of Detention were locked in theirs. The lights would go out at nine-thirty. The noise, the singing, the storytelling, the wildly vile language would go on until then. We were stunned by the impact of our reception, and the wild, maniacal spirits of all those young women about us. The week's work was finished, it was Friday night, and here were two days of leisure ahead. (I found out later that the tension had been increased by the quarantine of the women for two weeks before because of a case of diphtheria the doctor had brushed off for two or three days as malingering. For those two weeks the women had been idle and confined to a single floor during the hottest part of the summer, and not even allowed their hour a day on the roof.)

I thought of Salinger's story and I found it hard to excuse myself for my own immediate harsh reaction. It is all very well to hate the sin and love the sinner in theory, but it is hard to do in practice. By my peremptory rejection of the kind of welcome we received, I had, of course, protected Judith, but there was not expression of loving friendship in it. Lying there on my hard bed, I mourned to myself: "Jesus is the fat lady. Jesus is this Jackie who is making advances. Jesus is Baby Doll, her cellmate."

Jackie was released the next week; she had finished her six months, or her year, or her two years, or whatever it was. Baby Doll was one of those who risked being put in the "cooler," by waving and shouting to her friend from the window at the end of our corridor. From a window I watched Jackie, handsome and well dressed, hover a moment on the corner of the Avenue of the Americas and Tenth Street, then disappear into a bar. A week later, we saw in the *Daily News* (which can be purchased by the inmates) that Jackie had attempted suicide and had been taken to the Bellevue psychiatric prison ward. And a week after that she was back in the House of Detention, on another floor.

The other prisoners certainly did not harbor any hostility to us, nor take offense at the openness of my judgment. It was my interior fear and harshness that I was judging in myself.

Remembering Salinger, and Dostoevski's Father Zossima, and Alyosha, and the Honest Thief, and Tolstoi's short stories made me feel again that I had failed. We had the luxury of books; our horizons were widened though we were imprisoned. We could certainly not consider ourselves poor. Each day I read the prayers and lessons from my daily missal and breviary, which the priest brought me, and, when I told Judith stories of the fathers of the desert, she told me tales of the Hassidim. On the feast of St. Mary Magdalene I read:

> On my bed at night I sought him
> Whom my heart loves—
> I sought him but I did not find him.
>
> I will rise then and go about the city;
> In the streets and crossings I will seek
> Him whom my heart loves.
> I sought Him but I did not find him.
>
> Oh, that you were my brother,
> nursed at my mother's breasts!
> If I met you out of doors, I would kiss you
> and none would taunt me.
> I would lead you, bring you in
> to the home of my mother. . . .
>
> Rejoice with me, all you who love the Lord, for
> I sought him and he appeared to me. And while I
> was weeping at the tomb, I saw my Lord, Alleluia.

Yes, we fail in love, we make our judgments and we fail to see that we are all brothers; we are all seeking love, seeking God, seeking the beatific vision. All sin is a perversion, a turning from God and a turning to creatures. If only our love had been stronger and truer, casting out fear, I would not have taken the stand I did.

Suppose Judith *had* been Jackie's cellmate for the night, and suppose she had been able to convey a little of the strong, pure love the pacifists feel is the force which will overcome war: perhaps, perhaps—But this is the kind of analyzing and introspection and examination of conscience the narrator in *The Fall* did after he heard that cry in the dark, that splash in the Seine, and went on his way without having helped his brother, only to hear a mocking laughter that followed him ever after.

Thank God for retroactive prayer! St. Paul said that he did not judge himself, nor must we judge ourselves. We can turn to our Lord Jesus Christ, who has already repaired the greatest evil that ever happened or could ever happen, and trust that He will make up for our falls, for our neglects, for our failures in love.

Ammon Hennacy (fourth from left) and Dorothy Day (seventh from left, seated on bench) lead demonstration against atomic war in Washington Square.

Part V

Love
in Practice

< *Hans Tunneson, a Norwegian seaman, was responsible for building the chapel at Peter Maurin Farm. He came to the Catholic Worker in 1945, after getting out of a city hospital, and stayed, as he said, "to help the poor." At sea he earned his living as a cook, but now prefers carpentry. He also cooks, bakes, and teaches at the farm.*

Chapter 17

A Block Off the Bowery

THE CATHOLIC WORKER HAS HAD SO MANY HOMES, AND WE HAVE been forced to move so regularly, that we are almost used to it by now. (This is, I suppose, a part of our precarity which we must accept.) First there was Fifteenth Street, then, two years later, Charles Street, and then Mott Sreet, which we had rent-free and where we remained for fifteen years—our longest stay in any one place. But, following the war, our housing troubles began plaguing us once again. A month after Peter's death in 1949, we were given notice to move out of our Mott Street house. Miss Burke had also died, and the Chancery Office had ordered the House of Calvary to sell the buildings to raise money for a new wing on their hospital.

After much looking, disappointment, and prayer we were able to locate suitable new quarters—at 223 Chrystie Street—and to buy the building. It was the only home in the city we have ever owned; we paid $30,000 for it, and the bulk of this came from small donations.

The Catholic Worker group has never incorporated; since we wish to make a point of personal responsibility, the farms and houses we own have been in the name of one or another of us. For five years the house was in Tom Sullivan's name, but when he entered the Trappists for a trial of the monk's life, the house was transferred to my name. It was then the building inspectors started coming around, and we did our best to remedy whatever they complained about. But, without realizing it, we needed a lawyer, someone who knew the intricacies of the law and could interpret them to us. We got hopelessly mixed up as to what the inspectors meant when they said we were living in a "multiple dwelling" and had to file "plans," and by the time we hired an architect, as it turned out, it was too late. At that point I asked a friend of mine, Dorothy Tully, to act for us.

I thanked God I had our lawyer beside me when I had to answer a summons to appear in court on more charges of violating the building code. She, having just come onto the case, was as astounded as I was when the judge imposed on me a fine of $500 for being a slum landlord and operating a firetrap, a fine which he decreased a few moments later to $250, giving me two days to pay.

Our new St. Joseph's was now classified as a multiple dwelling, a hotel, and we were forced to satisfy the established official standards for such buildings. The City told us that the very fact that those who came to us could not pay entitled them all the more to building code protections, because they were really not free to go elsewhere.

The fact of the matter is that for the first time we had central heating, bathrooms and toilets on every floor, plenty of hot water for our washing, large, airy, sunny rooms, and so on. When we moved in there were no violations listed and we were given a certificate of occupancy. But now the housing inspector suddenly announced that there was already a "vacate notice" issued against us—to take effect the following Wednesday morning.

All this came as a most stunning blow. My first reaction was that on no account would I pay such a fine; I would rather go to jail instead. But then I thought of the fifty or more people who were dependent on the house for shelter and who would have to find homes within a week. I could see them being herded off to municipal shelters, mental hospitals, old age homes, the poor farm, hospitals on Welfare Island—to all the huge, cold institutions that break the spirit and the heart. Some of our family could be put on the relief rolls and be given furnished rooms and money for meals—that I knew—but many could only survive in a family such as ours. Neither the giant institutions nor the lonely isolation of furnished hall bedrooms would fit their case, nor would The Pioneer, a hotel for women on the Bowery, where single women are sent from the Family Shelter.

It was February 26 when we appeared in court. In two days the month of St. Joseph was to begin. All we could do was pray to him. And for a small-town carpenter (although a somewhat traveled man, what with his exile in Egypt) he certainly set the wheels in motion.

The first thing that happened was a call from Will Lissner of the *New York Times*, a star reporter (he always signs his articles) who understands Catholic social principles. He was telephoning on another matter altogether. I told him what had happened and he hastened down to see us. The fine, he said, seemed exorbitant. He visited through the house, called the judge and the Commissioner of Housing, and wrote a story about our crisis. His article must have led the judge to reconsider, for he phoned Miss Tully to come in with her client the next morning.

The news story also reached W. H. Auden, who had just been awarded the poetry chair at Oxford and who was soon leaving for England. With all the spontaneity and warmth of the true poet, Auden hurried down. He met me just as I was leaving the house on the way to the court at 151st Street. A group of men were already hanging around the entrance to St. Joseph's House to await the ten-o'clock distribution of clothes (after parcel post comes in). As Mr. Auden seemed to be stepping out of the group, I thought he was one of the unemployed who come to us, as they often do in snowy weather, to get extra clothing—overshoes, and such—that they need in order to work at clearing snow from the streets.

Many a distinguished man in unpressed tweeds, a bit drawn in the face from cold or from fatigue, has come to us with basic needs other than receiving loving-kindness. Just the same, I am still embarrassed at my mistake. I had been so harried that I could scarcely see, let alone identify anyone. Mr. Auden pressed a piece of paper into my hands and said, "Here is two-fifty." I truly thought it was $2.50 offered toward the fine. When I opened the paper in the subway and saw a $250 check with his name on it, I could have wept for joy. It was so beautiful a gesture.

When I appeared before the judge again that morning, he said he had not known we were a charitable institution and suspended the fine, giving us thirty day to get the work started to bring the place into line with the housing codes. When the building inspector grumbled that it would cost at least $28,000, the judge wanted to knew whether we thought we could manage it. I told him St. Joseph could. "Who is St. Joseph?" he asked. Mr. Brady, the inspector, answered that he was the saint to whom *he* prayed when he had to appear before Judge Nichol. "Does it do you any good?" the judge inquired. The inspector shook his head.

With all these visits to court, to municipal offices, lawyers, architects, and sprinkler men, Charles McCormack, who was manager and general treasurer of St. Joseph's House then, had a very busy time, taking most of the burden off my shoulders.

And through it all the men of the press were kind and courteous and sympathetic; their stories were in the same spirit. As a result, within two weeks $15,000 came in. We were able to get our work well under way—the work of installing a complete sprinkler system throughout the house, steel, self-closing doors, and all the other changes the city was calling for. We were somewhat discouraged to hear one inspector say that it would take closer to $40,000 than to $28,000; but, after all, we thought, the state spends far more on one guided missile. When we sent out our usual spring appeal, we had no doubt but that our bills would be covered, and our need for food, too.

I learned something as I sat in courts, overheated and stifling, and saw the crowded dockets, the masses of documents relating to a million minor offenses.

I saw that the system is all too big, too ponderous, too unwieldy. Everything needs to be decentralized, into many smaller institutions, smaller hospitals, courts, and so on. I wonder that there is ever any unemployment, with all the work that needs to be done in the world.

Well, the work was done; $24,000 was spent on the house and money was left over to pay off the mortgage on our Staten Island farm. We lived in peace and quiet for two years, in our renovated house, when suddenly the City sent everyone on our block notices to vacate because a subway was being dug beneath us, a connecting link between Delancey and Houston streets. Again we had to move.

We had to go back to renting and took a loft on Spring Street, nearby, in a long-established, clannish, solidly Italian community. Our neighbors objected strenuously to our moving in among them. The fact that we had lived for fifteen years only a few blocks south on Mott Street carried no weight with them—this was another "village." (Our landlord, Mr. Migliaccio, had a picture of the Blessed Virgin on one side of his desk and a photograph of Marilyn Monroe on the other. His brother, he once told me, had been a general in Mussolini's army.) We lived on Spring Street only a year and a half.

In September, 1960, the city finally paid us $68,700 for the Chrystie Street property, which had increased in value both as a result of our repairs and additions and because of the general increase in property values. When they sent us the check, they sent a second check, for interest accrued, in the amount of $3,579.39. As a matter of principle, we sent this back, with a long letter published on page 1 of the paper, outlining our reasons for doing so. It included the following paragraph:

We are returning the interest on the money we have recently received because we do not believe in "money-lending at interest." As Catholics we are acquainted with the early teaching of the Church. All the early Councils forbade it, declaring it reprehensible to make money by lending it out at interest. . . .

In the same issue we ran a column setting forth the views of St. Thomas on usury, as well as an Easy Essay called "Banking on Bankers." And the same month Ammon and four others picketed the national convention of the American Bankers' Association at the Waldorf-Astoria. One of their signs read:

We got a number of letters from readers criticizing our act, and in the next issue I defended our position as best I could.

We spent all the principal within the year on our two beach bungalows, a heating system for the farm on Staten Island and its outbuildings, and in many gifts to needy families.

Our last move—as of this writing—was occasioned by orders from the Fire, Building, and Health Departments, and it took us from Spring back to Chrystie Street, north of Delancey, a block off the Bowery, only two blocks from our former home. Now we have a three-story building for which we pay a very high rent but which is working out quite satisfactorily.

Today St. Joseph's House of Hospitality, sandwiched in among tenements, looks brighter since Walter Karell painted the bricks above the doorway with gay enamel. ("The green shows up most on rainy days," says Walter, "but the sunshine brings out the yellows and the reds.")

On the first floor are our dining room and kitchen; this floor becomes a meeting room on Friday nights. On the second floor is a long sitting room where men and women from the neighborhood can rest and read or just sit. Two weeks of a month it becomes a busy place when everyone helps us mail out the paper.

When it isn't crowded you can see the walls with their shelves of papers and magazines and books, the two weaving looms—one of them homemade—the attractive pictures on the walls. In the two windows are statues of St. Joseph carved from a stone doorstep by Joseph O'Connell, a Minnesota artist and St. Francis, carved by Umlauf, a Texan. Besides these good things, the overall bareness is also relieved by occasional gaudy little shrines tucked here and there, put up by one or another of our guests.

At the back of the second floor are the two rooms where we give out clothes, one for women, one for men. The former is

usually crowded with Puerto Rican mothers and their children looking over the contribution of garments which they need so badly. We seldom have enough clothes for the men, and we are likely to have more coats than trousers. On the third floor we have our offices, with six desks, a few tables and typewriters, a bookcase and filing cabinets.

Facing as it does the open space across the street, St. Joseph's is bright and sunny. Much hard work on everyone's part has made it a bit cleaner, and it is not unattractive. Here we feed our guests and do our work, not infrequently spending twelve hours a day.

Besides the house on Chrystie Street, we have ten apartments of two to four rooms each where "the family" is housed, most of them on Spring Street and Kenmare nearby. Some of the apartments are primitive: bathtub next to the kitchen sink; hot water but as yet no heat; toilet in the hall. Our neighbors are Chinese, Puerto Rican, Negro, and Italian, with an overflow of young people from Greenwich Village, to the northwest of us.

On the whole we are pleased with the house on Chrystie Street; yet we know too that this home is a temporary one. All over New York, slums are being torn down to make way for housing projects. It is getting harder and harder to be poor. When we are forced to move again, we have no notion where we may go. We will face that day when it comes.

In many cities, houses of hospitality are still functioning effectively today. A diocesan house in Portland, Oregon, feeds a thousand men or so a day and runs both a very good hotel and a refuge for men just out of prison. The first house in San Francisco closed down, but another started up in Oakland across the bay, run first by an intellectual ex-hotel clerk, then by a poet, William Everson. Bill became a Catholic while he was in a camp for conscientious objectors during the war, later joining the Dominicans. He writes remarkable verse under the name of Brother Antoninus. He has been in great demand (as a spiritual counselor) among the beats of the West Coast. His lectures are so well attended, so I have been told, that the West Coast bishops indicated gently that they wouldn't mind his accepting lecture engagements in other parts of the country, if he would keep quiet around home.

The Oakland house was continued by Carroll McCool, an ex-Marine and an ex-Trappist. He was not an intellectual, but he understood the men and they understood him. He kept a neat, efficient house, where he fed from eight hundred to a thousand men a day and lodged forty. With all that, he said the rosary constantly; it was never out of his hands.

Once, when I visited him on a trip to the West Coast, he had been given a hard time by one of the men the night before. The man, according to one of the cooks, had raged through the house brandishing a knife and threatening wholesale slaughter.

"And how did Carroll handle him?" I wanted to know.

"Oh," said the cook, smiling, "he just sat over there in that rocking chair and said his rosary and bowed his head until the storm blew over."

I asked where the one-man riot was now. The cook pointed him out—a hulking fellow quietly waiting on table, his hand a bit shaky and spilling the soup now and then, but calmed down, sobered, peaceable.

Here was an outstanding example on the part of an ex-Marine of nonviolent resistance to violence, hatred, and imminent murder. Although he had gone through religious conversion, he knew nothing about Gandhi or Vinoba Bhave and probably didn't even read *The Catholic Worker* (despite the fact that it was sent to him by the bundle!).

I was told, however, that he never hesitated to refuse entry to someone who was likely to cause trouble, or to eject anyone who was still rational enough to understand what he was saying. He had both moral force and the physical force to back it up; the fact that he refrained from using the physical only earned him the greater respect in the eyes of the men.

"Use your common sense as far as it will take you," Father Roy used to say, "and, when you realize you can do nothing, bow your head to the storm and pray—pray without ceasing.

If that fails, rejoice that you, too, are accounted worthy to suffer and to realize your weakness and keep on praying like the importunate widow."

That Oakland house, in a rented building, was recently closed down to make way for "urban renewal," which we know only as demolition. But another has already started up, the St. Elijah House.

Still another West Coast project, though not literally a house of hospitality, has the same purpose. A group in Tracy, California, got under way when one family, who could have lived in bourgeois comfort, moved in among the Negro and Mexican agricultural workers. The husband works on the railroad to pay their way, and the wife serves the neighborhood—not as a professional social worker but as a stimulator of mutual aid. They are surrounded by bracero camps, the nearest thing to the Russian slave labor camps we can boast of. The men are paid, it is true, but they live under miserable conditions. They are separated from their pay by every means that can be devised. In some sections women are imported on pay nights for these men, who have been shipped up like machines for the harvest and are separated from their families.

Our experiences in the Midwest have varied. The house in St. Louis closed, but the group continued to function, two of whom published a paper, *The Living Parish*. Others have opened a combination art center and bookstore where they hold discussion meetings Friday evenings.

In Chicago, houses of hospitality have had a checkered history. The largest one closed in the early years of the war, but was quickly followed by another, staffed by some conscientious objectors who worked in the Alexian Brothers Hospital. But this house was frowned upon by the hierarchy. We were in the war, it was argued, and to try to talk pacifism and conscientious objection was not only un-American but un-Catholic.

This house was quickly closed, but another one called "Peter Maurin House" opened after the war. Although the original group who started it has dispersed, it is still operating. This house has never been concerned with positions or stands, but day after day it feeds the hungry and houses the homeless.

Now there are two others in Chicago, one called "St. Stephen's House of Hospitality," on West Oak Street, and another on Mohawk, run by Karl Meyer, who went to jail with us in New York and went on the San Francisco-to-Moscow Peace Walk. Karl stresses voluntary poverty and personal responsibility. The house is small, and he emphasizes the need to remain small in order to illustrate the point that such a life as they lead there is both possible and necessary today. Karl considers the activities at St. Stephen's a work for peace, just as he does his march from Chicago to Moscow.

In Detroit, the efforts of Louis Murphy are evidence that a family can undertake works of mercy and raise their own children in a slum, not only without their being contaminated, but on the contrary demonstrating an ability to lift the level of intelligence and awareness of the other children in the neighborhood. Louis runs a St. Francis House for men and a St. Martha House for women and has remained faithful to the work for more than twenty-five years.

The Washington, D.C., house of hospitality is having its troubles. This one-man venture, managed by a Negro, Llewellyn Scott, is being dispossessed to make room for urban renewal. Llewellyn is now engaged in the heartbreaking search for new quarters, seeking a neighborhood that will put up with the poor and the destitute—both black and white—who come to him.

In Pittsburgh, a house of hospitality is still functioning—it has become a diocesan house—in an old orphanage in the Hill district.

I never fail to be touched when I visit the Cleveland house of hospitality, which has moved to the country. There, Bill Gauchat and his wife, although they have six children of their own, care for as many as seven neglected children at a time—sufferers from multiple sclerosis, cerebral palsy, and other trying diseases of mind and body. I will always remember the picture of the Gouchats' home last Christmas season. Some of the distorted little ones were lying on the floor, gazing with radiant faces at the lighted tree and listening to the carols Dorothy Gauchat was playing for them on the record player.

The house in Rochester still goes on, and so does the old argument between pacifists and nonpacifists there. The house in Boston was taken over to provide a home for the Brothers of St. John of God. They would have kept it going, but were unable to meet the building requirements of the city.

The houses of hospitality have remained from the start one of the cornerstones of The Catholic Worker movement, as they were a cornerstone of Peter Maurin's original program.

The city, the state—we have nicknamed them Holy Mother the City, Holy Mother the State—have taken on a large role in sheltering the homeless. But the ideal is for every family to have a Christ room, as the early fathers of the Church called it. The prophets of Israel certainly emphasized hospitality. It seems to me that in the future the family—the ideal family—will always try to care for one more. If every family that professed to follow Scriptural teaching, whether Jew, Protestant, or Catholic, were to do this, there would be no need for huge institutions, houses of dead storage where human beings waste away in loneliness and despair. Responsibility must return to the parish with a hospice and a center for mutual aid, to the group, to the family, to the individual.

One reason I feel sure of the rightness of the path we are traveling in our work is that we did not pick it out ourselves. In those beautiful verses in the twenty-fifth chapter of St. Matthew, Jesus tells us that we must feed the hungry, and shelter those without homes and visit the sick and the prisoner. We cannot feel too satisfied with the way we are doing our work—there is too much of it; we have more than our share, you might say. Yet we can say, "If that's the way He wants it—"

I say we did not choose this work, and that is true. So it was with each of us. John Cort thought he was coming to us to study and work with the problem of labor unions and he found himself "running a flophouse," as he said. I, being a journalist, looked to editing and publishing a paper each month, writing what I chose, and not being subject to any publisher. But because we wrote about the obligations of those who call themselves Christians and who try "stripping yourselves of the old man with his deeds and putting on the new," as St. Paul said, it is as though we were each being admonished, "All right, if you believe as you say, do it."

One time, as I was standing at the window of our farmhouse at Newburgh, I saw a man coming down the road with a suitcase. "He is probably coming here," I sighed. Another member of the family turned to me accusingly and said, "Then you don't *mean* what you say in *The Catholic Worker!*"

"Is this what you meant, Peter?" I asked him once about an overcrowded house of hospitality.

"Well," he hesitated. "At least it arouses the conscience."

Which is something.

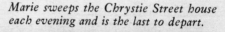

Marie sweeps the Chrystie Street house each evening and is the last to depart.

Chapter 18

Peter Maurin Farm

WHEN THE WORLD IS TOO MUCH WITH ME, OR WHEN I WANT TO go on retreat, I can always slip away for a few days to Peter Maurin Farm on Staten Island. I never tire of the trip—whether by bus or our old car, which is always on the point of giving up —down the East Side to the ferry, across the harbor, then out on the island to the farm.

It is a fine sight to see the skyscrapers of Manhattan slip away astern; with them fade the cares and clangor of the city. The salt spray is fresh; the ships we pass speak to us of far places. Landing on the other side, we are caught by traffic again; but mile by mile it thins out. We turn off the main road onto a side road that goes up over one little hill and through the woods, and soon we are at the farm.

The buildings themselves are not impressive in appearance: a brown-shingled farmhouse, sagging somewhat and falling apart at the seams; a barn with the cross on the side that is now our little chapel; a row of little rooms made from a carriage shed; carpenter shops; a chicken coop; and, at the foot of the hill, a duck pond which is claimed right now by a flock of geese.

But we have twenty-two acres of good land on which we raise over a thousand quarts of tomatoes—land on which we pay $1,500 a year in taxes. It is, after all, a farm in New York City!

Inside, the house has the peaceful air of an old-fashioned family farmhouse. I never know what members of our "family" I will find here. Today there is an old newspaperman who has come to stay with us while he recovers from a long illness; a pretty young girl who is pregnant, and whose family doesn't know it; a man who sits quietly in a corner trying to get over a spree on the Bowery; a Negro girl from the South and her two little children.

Then there are the regulars: our "hermit," for example, who isn't exactly antisocial but likes to be left alone. He lives in a shack by himself down in the woods. Then there is Agnes, in her eighties now. From upstairs, I hear the thump of Stanley's printing press; he may be printing some prayer cards for us, or marriage or baptismal announcements. Larry, who has been with us for years in the city, is in the kitchen in the basement, cooking up a stew for dinner; Classie Mae, a Negro girl, takes over for him one day a week, and Hans on Sundays.

Jean Walsh is in charge of the house, succeeding Beth Rogers, who ran it for ten years. Beth now lives in an apartment in town, devoting herself to the care of a blind friend who is suffering from ulcerated legs.

Jean, a trained nurse, has saved one life—literally—and prolonged and eased many others in the few years she has been with us. Coming from a well-to-do family, she has the smallest room in the house and the fewest belongings. She is steadily divesting herself of what she has in order to give to others.

Among our family are those so afflicted by ill health of mind or body that they cannot earn a living in the world outside, and yet they look after others who are more handicapped. They suffer and they serve, each in his own way.

We have had our trials at Peter Maurin Farm, as we have had at Chrystie Street. On the day after Labor Day a couple of years ago, the holiday guests having gone, we were straightening up the house when a car drove up to the front door. Two men got out. They looked the house over; then they came slowly and ominously inside the privet hedge, onto the grassy lawn where the littlest children had had such a lovely time all summer, playing croquet or splashing in a rubber pool given us by a neighbor. Standing under the tall pine tree which had shaded many an invalid from the city, as he sat happily watching

Peter Maurin Farm on Staten Island,
rear view of the buildings. Left, the main house.
At right is the rebuilt barn which houses the chapel.

the antics of babies just learning to walk, the strangers announced themselves.

"We are from the Building Department."

About ten days before, we had received a notice from the Department. Since ours was a frame building, the notice read, and was classified as a multiple dwelling, it altogether violated the law and could not be repaired and renovated, as St. Joseph's house in Chrystie Street had been. Their orders to us were to reconvert into a one-family house.

The inspectors were in a cold, implacable mood—or so it seemed to me. Probably they didn't like the job before them, which was to go over the place and see if we were obeying their orders, and, if we were not, to issue a summons.

We told them that we were complying with their instructions and request, that the house was being vacated as a multiple dwelling. Only the night before, Frances Ferguson had gone into town, Orletta Ryan had returned to Chicago, Philip had packed up ready to vacate his attic, Howard and Peggy were all packed to leave, Stanley was in Canada. The only ones living in the house were Agnes Sidney, Magdalene and her two children, and myself. And this in a house of eleven rooms, with two attics and two baths!

The men wanted to know whether we were a group under Catholic auspices. We told them that we had a visiting priest who was at present ill in St. Vincent's Hospital, that the Blessed Sacrament was reserved in our barn chapel, and that Father Guerin, or Father Mailleux of the Marist fathers, came often to offer Mass, and once a month we had a day of recollection. When they wanted to know what the word "Worker" meant, we reminded them (I believe they were Catholics) that the Labor Day Mass at the Cathedral in New York had been in honor of St. Joseph *the Worker*. (Later they took a few copies of the paper with them.)

They went around the house, measuring, calling out the location of doors, windows, alcoves; then they went inside, into every room from attic to cellar. Finally they came down to inform us that they had found two mattresses stored in the attic. "They will have to be removed." We agreed to burn them. No, that was not necessary. They seemed to think I was almost too drastic. They could be stored elsewhere. And then they asked, "But who are all these people?" The girl they saw, I explained, was a neighbor, who brought her three little children to meals with us because her husband was in the hospital with blood poisoning. The other two young girls outside stringing beads were visitors from Friendship House, New York.

They poked around some more.

"Why are these tables in the dining room and kitchen?" they asked suspiciously. "It looks as though you were feeding a lot of people." I explained that on Sundays we had days of recollection and many people came down to spend the day and listen to conferences.

"Well, you may be getting into trouble for that," said one, "making this a place of assembly."

Was there any way we could live, I wondered, was there

anything we could do, which would *not* get us into trouble?

As the two men left, they looked over the green fields, the rows of corn, the field of tomatoes. "What about that big oven you had where you were baking bread?" they asked. I told them that we no longer had the oven. We had given it away. We only baked bread for ourselves now. "And what will you do about the farm? Will you keep on working it?" Yes, we would raise all the vegetables we could to feed ourselves and others in New York who came to eat at our table. And where would the farmer live? Why, in his cabin near the carpenter shop.

"We will have to look into that next" was their parting remark.

We were indignant. We are not a slum. The neighbors are proud of our farm. Visitors think of our place as a foretaste of Heaven, a little bit of Paradise, with its grove in the woods for conferences, its meditation places down by the brook, its stations of the cross inside the chapel and outside, down the wagon track through the fields.

This house and farm cost $16,000 in 1950. We have rejoiced in the twenty-two acres around us, the fields and the woods where we have grown so much food and provided healthful work of one sort or another for so many otherwise unemployable, and given the opportunity, too, for the practice of the works of mercy, and the living-in-community.

For the first time in the thirty years of The Catholic Worker, we have inside plumbing on a farm. (At Easton, Pennsylvania, and at Maryfarm, Newburgh, there were outhouses which were painted, moved each year, and kept in good condition. It is permissible for the Army to provide such buildings, I understand, but not for us.) Here at Peter Maurin Farm, we have a bath and toilet in the house on both floors, central heating, and a plumbing system which gives plenty of hot water for washing and bathing. The house is an old shingled farmhouse, formerly owned by a Swiss family who farmed it profitably in asparagus, corn, and strawberries. They kept a cow, a horse, and chickens, and had grapes from which they made their own wine, and there was a good well predating the city water supply.

What, I ask myself, are they doing to us in the name of public safety—and why?

Yes, there are problems in ownership as well as in poverty and destitution. Every day we face the kind of situation the inspectors could never understand. This noon, for example, someone called to ask if we would take in a sixteen-year-old girl who was going to have a baby. She was still with her parents; her father was willing to help her, but her mother was making life unbearable. The girl had already tried to commit suicide by climbing out on a ledge of their apartment. Her friends were looking for some place for the girl to stay temporarily, until they could see what might best be done. Despite all this housing trouble, I could not refuse. We have plenty of space even within this ruling that limits us to one family and four roomers. I can stay in New York, and she can be one of the roomers. When I come out to spend the night, I come as a guest. I wonder if each of us is permitted to have a guest, and how often, and for how long.

It is a strange and terrifying business, this all-encroaching state, when it interferes to such a degree in the personal practice of the works of mercy. How terrible a thing it is when the state takes over the poor! "State ownership of the indigent," one of the bishops called it. The authorities want us to live according to certain standards, or not at all. We are forced to raise our standard of living, regardless of the debts involved. We are forced to be institutional, which is not what we want.

How to escape from the letter of the law that killeth! Our lawyer says that there is nothing we can do in the end but move to Vermont or to one of the Southern states. But there in the South we would get into great trouble because of our stand on the racial issue. There is no easy living for a Christian in this world!

Peter Maurin Farm is the most recent of the farming communes which came into being as a result of The Catholic Worker movement. It is true that many such farms do exist today, but they evolved into family farms rather than the farming communes which Peter envisioned. Some are in the hands of from three to six families. More often a single family, because of its large number of children, has stayed on a farm to run it alone after others have left. We are always hearing of this through visitors who come to us in New York. But I hesitate to name their localities, because there is such a hunger for community, there are so many wandering monks and scholars (those whom Tolstoi's overburdened wife called "the dark ones"), that I would not want to be responsible for disturbing their privacy.

After we sold one of our two farms at Easton to a neighboring family, we bought another farm at Newburgh, New York. We were happy there until the jet planes from a nearby airbase disturbed our retreats so greatly that we had to move again. It was then we bought the farm on Staten Island.

Our farm home today is not large, but it still has some of the elements both of a farming commune and of an agronomic university. We have people there who can preserve, who can bake, who can letter and illuminate, who are good carpenters, electricians, and plumbers. Hans Tunnesen, a Norwegian seaman, built our chapel, but he also bakes bread, cooks for our feasts, and has taught others to do the same. Joe Roche, who was crippled in an accident for which he received no compensation, is still able to work around kitchen and laundry. Joe Cotter, our electrician, cans thousands of quarts of vegetables from our truck garden each summer.

If we have failed to achieve Peter's ideals, it is perhaps because we have tried to be all things to all men: to run a school, an agronomic university, a retreat house, an old people's home, a shelter for delinquent boys and expectant mothers, a graduate school for the study of communities, of religions, of man and the state, of war and peace. We have aimed high; and we hope we have accomplished enough at least "to arouse the conscience." Here is the way—or rather here is *a* way—for those who love God and their neighbor to try to live by the two great commandments. The frustrations that we experience are exercises in faith and hope, which are supernatural virtues. With prayer, one can go on cheerfully and even happily. Without prayer, how grim a journey!

When people try living and working together voluntarily, they naturally create many problems that try the patience. I think of little things that can easily assume the proportions of big ones.

Just now our farmer, who has been with us for twenty-three years, has plowed up a field of corn and a garden of unripe tomatoes purely out of an impulse to use the tractor, which he loves, and to restore the untidy field to neat, orderly rows. It hurts me to think of the green tomatoes that would have been ripening until Thanksgiving, of the late corn which could have been dried and fed to the pigs.

Dick Barber washes jars at Peter Maurin Farm. More than a thousand quarts of tomatoes were canned in 1962 for use at the House of Hospitality on Chrystie Street.

And the difficulties in hanging on to property!

I remember the time when we had just bought the farm and Harold, cleaning the barn, threw out a lot of rusty tools which he, being a man of the age of automation, did not recognize. Some, rescued from the trash, turned out to be museum pieces. These were saved, but how many were lost!

And the time when Hester, in an orgy of housecleaning, tossed out handspun, handwoven blankets because they were a little frayed around the edges.

And the time when a college boy who was so generous as to give up his bed to a stranger rolled himself up to sleep on the floor in what he took to be a blanket. In the morning I found him sleeping in a most precious Paisley shawl. We rescued it and used it as an altar covering in the chapel. In the end it vanished—no one knows where.

The farm library is open to all our guests. Autographed copies of books by Maritain, Eric Gill, and Belloc disappear. A friend carved us some beautiful statues and crucifixes, and one night they were gone. Another friend gave us a tapestry, a copy of a famous painting. Someone looked upon it with desire and it was gone, too. Living in common as we do, available to all, free to all, we expect these things to happen. As Peter used to say when he found an animal neglected, or the engine of a car frozen because someone had forgotten to drain the water out of it, "Everyone's property is no one's property." Neglect and abuse— these are failings common to all classes of society, particularly in this most prosperous land of ours, where we have built an economy on waste.

The same farmer who plowed up the field once told me how, on a farm where he worked in New England, if a cow was hard to dry up before the new calf came, the farmer had only to milk her onto the ground and she became so enraged at the waste that she dried up at once.

I am afraid that nature may become similarly enraged at our own waste here in our too blessed America. You see it on every hand: in the Army, in the jails, in all public institutions. Even the school lunch system gives evidence of it. Corporations hire efficiency engineers to eliminate waste motions and thus help them save a few pennies; unions fight and strike to get a few cents an hour wage increase for their workers. At the same time there is wanton waste everywhere, on the part of every man, woman, and child.

One can only admire the vision and tenacity of those in public life who, against such discouraging odds, persevere in working for the common good. "What doesn't belong to them they are careless of," Peter would say. Which to his way of thinking was an argument not against communal ownership of the means of production but for a better understanding of the doctrine of the common good and a need for the growth in co-operatives—manageable ones of proper size, so that each could have a sense of personal responsibility.

Faced with such irresponsibility, ignorance, greed, envy, sloth (one could list a few more of the deadly sins which I see around me on the farm, as well as in the world as a whole), I am often almost discouraged, but then I remember to go over to the chapel to pray for patience, for a restoration of inner peace.

It takes some time to calm one's heart, which fills all too easily with irritation, resentment, and anger. But there, in the quiet of the chapel, looking around at the work done by those same men who caused the irritation, it is easier to adjust one's thoughts. It is all right to condemn the waste, but, on the other hand, one must keep in mind the necessity of loving the sinner while condemning the sin. I had to remind myself that the same sinner who plowed under the crops had taught my little daughter to love the land. Many a day had she followed him as he plowed and harvested, gathering up the fruits, finding nests of field mice or baby rabbits. I thought of her riding on top of a load of hay and learning to milk the cow and the goats.

As I recalled how our farmer loved the fields and the earth, and transplanted tree and bush from the woods, all these recollections made me begin to shift the blame to myself. What might he have done had he been given proper direction or cooperation? He had never been asked to work to the limits of his strength or abilities. There was too little challenge for him in the small work we were accomplishing. He should have been part of a larger acreage where men worked from dawn until dark, and together saw great things being accomplished. When I think of the *kibbutzim* in Israel, and the reclaiming of the desert, and the reforestation of bare hillsides, how feeble all our efforts over these past twenty-eight years seem by comparison. How little we have attempted, let alone accomplished.

The consolation is this—and this our faith too: By our suffering and our failures, by our acceptance of the Cross, by our struggle to grow in faith, hope, and charity, we unleash forces that help to overcome the evil in the world.

It is good to be able to see things in this perspective and to laugh with others who laugh at us when they see our "Brother Juniper" attempts at social reform. Our farmer's failures are our own; but we must forgive ourselves as well as him. Thinking about all his work and goodness, my criticism turns to gratitude and love, and so my heart is warmed and I am comforted.

Chapter 19

Our Day

IN THE MORNING THINGS ARE BRISK AT CHRYSTIE STREET. CHARLIE or Ed or Walter is planning the meals, making out the order for the grocer (not a chain store) with whom we have traded for the past twenty-five years. Italian Mike is getting ready to take his old aluminum frame of a baby carriage down to the bakery or the fish market to bring back boxes of food for the day. He literally walks miles on such errands. He is the earliest riser and sweeps not only our own sidewalk but the sidewalk for the entire block. Everybody in the neighborhood knows Mike and appreciates him. One might say he is our public relations man.

Through the windows running all across the front of the building we can look across the street to the broad playground, and above that to a great expanse of sky that lifts up our hearts. Yes, in the morning things look good and cheerful. In the kitchen one man is peeling vegetables; another is finishing up some dishes at the high stainless-steel sinks. This fellow is an ailing seaman, who once brought me a kimono from Hong Kong. He has leukemia, but he wants to stay out of the hospital as long as he can.

We never ask people why they are here. They just come in from the streets to eat, to wait, to find some place for themselves, to have someone to talk to, someone with whom to share and so to lighten their troubles.

Bill gives me coffee, and George, the German waiter, rushes to get the good pumpernickel bread he has put aside for me. There is margerine, of course. One woman sitting at the table with me likes to have sliced onion with her bread. Someone else varies his diet with mustard. Once in a while we have donations of peanut butter and jam. We buy day-old bread; but now and then a seminary such as Maryknoll will bring a truckful of bread and other supplies (and in the fall a load of apples from their orchard). Bread and coffee and tea—these are the old standbys. The latter are necessary psychologically, though, as Peter Maurin always contended, soup is more nourishing.

Today, as I write, it is a sunny winter morning. I have just returned from a speaking trip to Notre Dame, Immaculata High School and adjoining Marygrove College in Detroit, Wayne State, and other colleges in the Midwest. What a relief it was —no phones to answer, no decisions to make. If I began worrying about responsibilities at home, Father McSorley's words would come back to me: "Go where you are invited," he used to say to me, simply, and my parish priest has often repeated the same advice. The long night ride home on the bus, perhaps because it was such a change from the routine, I found restful and beautiful.

Yet it is good to be back, too. Suddenly, again, there is the usual hurly burly of activity around me. Both phones seem to be ringing at once. Although it is still two hours before lunch, there is already a gathering of men, waiting patiently. So that they will no longer have to wait on the street, exposed to the curious eyes of the passersby, we have rented a big machine shop in the rear, where there are benches and a lavatory and where some of the "beats" have painted dancing and singing figures on the wall. They might better have whitewashed the place, I think to myself; some Tom Sawyer should come along and make such work attractive.

One does not do much leisurely thinking in St. Joseph's House of Hospitality. There is too much noise. Right now there is a Polish woman—who even at this early hour has already had too much to drink—screaming curses. For the sake of the common good, Charlie is trying to keep her out, but now, because of the cold, he has relented. He urges her to sit down and rest

*The second floor of the Chrystie Street house, where 70,000
copies of* The Catholic Worker
are mailed out every month.

and be quiet. I can see now that she will be a problem all day—
in again, out again, many times.

Up the short flight of stairs, on the second floor, it is no quieter.
At the end of the long table nearest the broad expanse of windows,
a few men and women sit, smoking and visiting in the cold
sunlight. There are others at the table, too, reading, writing
letters. At the dark end of the room, where a 150-watt electric
bulb burns all day, some girls are helping Anne Marie sort out
clothes. Arthur J. Lacey (called by some "the Bishop" because
of the prominent cross he wears on a chain around his neck, and
by others "Dear Soul," his own greeting to customers for men's
clothing) is boasting of the neatness of his clothes room.

But what bothers me about this second floor is the sight of
sacks and sacks of mail bags piled against the wall. These are the
letters for the semi-annual appeal. They should have gone to the
post office before this. Keith, who has taken care of the addresso-
graph and mailing room for the past ten years, intercepts me.
"Will you please tell Charlie hereafter to put aside enough money
from this appeal so that we will be able to mail it out."

I realize that within the next few days the new edition of *The Catholic Worker* (thank God it is only a monthly) will be brought in—seventy-three bundles, a thousand papers in each bundle. Everybody will be getting to work on it, folding, applying stickers, tying up bundles according to cities and states, then filling up more mail bags. But the appeal letters must be got out of the way first, to get the money to make the deposit at the P.O., to mail the paper out.

Charlie is upstairs in the office on the third floor, going over the checkbook and surveying a pile of bills neatly stacked on his desk. "The appeal couldn't go out because we didn't have five hundred dollars for stamps," he explains. Since the paper and printing for the appeal letter are donated, and since everyone joins in the labor of folding and stuffing envelopes for mailing, the stamps are the only expense. The money that comes in response is used directly for works of mercy—no salaries come out of it.

"We haven't got money for stamps?" I ask.

"Only forty dollars in the bank," he answers.

Forty dollars in the bank, and hundreds of people coming to the door to be fed each day. More than a thousand dollars in rents to be paid. Not to mention gas, electricity, telephone, heat. "Never be afraid to run up bills for the poor," Pope Pius XII told a community of nuns once. (Fortunately Tony, being an independent grocer, lets us run up our bills to five thousand dollars. Not so, corporations. Once our printer wrote on the bottom of the monthly bill, "Pray—and pay!")

I sit at my desk and begin opening the mail. The first several envelopes contain bills and I add them to the pile. The next envelope contains a check for $500!

Now the mail bags can get out and no time need be lost. Ours is a labor bank on Union Square and the officials have known us for thirty years. "Just go and explain our need," I tell Charlie, "and get the cash at once. They will give it to you, and then you can get the stamps."

Charlie leaves. An hour later he is back. "The check was made out wrong!" he tells me, and my heart sinks. "The numbers

'$500' were right, but it was written out 'five and no hundredths dollars.'

"They didn't take it?"

"I told him how desperately we needed it, and that the same person had donated large amounts in the past.. They finally took it! I have the stamps right here!"

We are all relieved, everyone works overtime, and the decks are soon cleared for action on the next issue of the paper. Needless to say, the appeal will bring in just enough barely to cover our bills. If we run short, we will have to take it as a lesson in precarity and draw in our belts. Wishing us to be like the poor, and taking us at our word when we speak of voluntary poverty, the Lord always leaves a few debts to worry us.

The morning mail also brings letters from Africa, India, Cuba, South America, France and England. And people are dropping in as usual; a seaman wanting to talk about the longshoremen's strike; some students reluctant to register for the draft and some who, though willing to register, are wondering about the Papal Peace Corps or President Kennedy's Peace Corps; students who want to know what kind of social order would prevail under anarchism, and whether we at the Catholic Worker deny *all* authority. The text most often quoted to us in argument against our concept of civil disobedience is "Render therefore to Caesar the things that are Caesar's; and to God, the things that are God's." If the discussion concerns pacifism, our opponents point up Christ's scourging the money changers out of the temple. The use of force and the necessity for the State are the two questions uppermost in the minds of the students.

Thirty years ago people's main problem was unemployment and the resulting depression. Then the war came, and with it, full employment. In the thirties there had been the Sino-Japanese war, the Ethiopian war, the Spanish Civil war; and in those years, too, we demonstrated against war. When the Second World War came and so few were left around to do the work, there was an end to peace demonstrations but no end to the discussion of war in the pages of *The Catholic Worker*. We still quoted the

Sermon on the Mount; we still spoke of the works of mercy and called attention to the fact that war is inevitably the opposite of them. Laying waste the fields, it brings famine; destroying homes, instead of sheltering the harborless, it drives people even out of their own country. ("You know not of what spirit you are," Jesus sadly told His apostles when they wanted to call down fire on the Samaritans who had refused them hospitality.)

Yes, we still oppose war and the preparations for it. And we are still on the side of the working man. Outwardly, things have changed for him, but "prosperity" and the age of automation have brought the situation almost full circle to what it was in the thirties. We have again today what Michael Harrington, one of our former editors, calls a "Second America": the America of the poor, now based on the unemployability of masses of men thrown out of work by the machine, or men unable to find a job because they are too old or young, insufficiently trained, mentally, unstable, or physically handicapped. And we do what we can to alleviate the suffering of this unemployment, which no war, hot or cold, will help.

Peter Maurin's teaching—his philosophy of work, his stress on the need for farming communes and agronomic universities—has yet to be applied to the problems of unemployment and automation. Much of the world has changed to a new society where collective and communal ownership is being emphasized to handle the matter of man and his work. But these changes have been brought about by violence and coercion, at the expense of man's freedom.

The greatest challenge of the day is: how to bring about a revolution of the heart, a revolution which has to start with each one of us? When we begin to take the lowest place, to wash the feet of others, to love our brothers with that burning love, that passion, which led to the Cross, then we can truly say, "Now I have begun."

Day after day we accept our failure, but we accept it because of our knowledge of the victory of the Cross. God has given us our vocation, as he gave it to the small boy who contributed his few loaves and fishes to help feed the multitude, and which

Jesus multiplied so that he fed five thousand people.

Loaves and fishes! How much we owe to God in praise, honor, thanksgiving! In our neighborhood the church bells ring at seven, eight and nine o'clock. Every day we go to whichever Mass is most convenient, and a few stay for awhile for a thanksgiving. Then at one o'clock or two, after the soup line is finished and the staff have had their more leisurely bowl, Millie rings a little bell. Those who wish say the Rosary together, the younger kneeling and the older sitting. Ukrainian Michael sways while he prays and is usually ten words ahead of anyone else.

Margaret used to rock in the one rocking chair, which was conceded to be hers. When little Margaret first came to us, it was with a shopping bag containing all her belongings. She told me how, little by little, she had gone down in the world— from running a furnished rooming-house, to living herself in a small furnished room, and then, finally, being evicted from that. Turned down by the City social workers on some technicality when she applied for relief, she slept in the subway for a few nights until a friendly priest found her and sent her to us. When she came, she was so fatigued that she stayed in bed for a week and ate voraciously everything offered her. After recovering her strength, she never spent another day in bed until the last week of her life. She helped us by braiding rugs out of old neckties, and by taking care of the clothing room several hours a day.

The Rosary said, we settle down for a few hours' work before the dinner crowd begins to come in. It will be more noisy and undisciplined than the noon crowd from the Bowery, including as it does all the staff and their friends, many of the latter being members of other peace groups who use our place to store their signs and get a hot meal. Whenever there is a specially fragrant dish cooking, such as pork chops or Italian sausage, the tantalizing odor spreads far and wide. The news seems to travel by grapevine. Then sometimes more people turn up than we have chops or sausage for, and we have recourse to soup again. Which means everybody crowds onto the first floor at once, hoping to secure the next place at table. "Always room for one more."

Benches and battered chairs line the brightly painted room.

The two long tables are set by German George; Charlie (or Ed or Walter) presides behind his serving table; pots are steaming on the stove; an opened oven door gives off a delicious smell. In summer, the side door lets in a good breeze. A Chinese philosophy student comes to us from around the corner on Mott Street, usually eats in silence, then leaves. A visiting priest from the Midwest may find himself trying to converse with a newly arrived Puerto Rican couple who know little English, at the same time passing the bread to a university intellectual who has come to write a paper on The Catholic Worker. A number of Negroes come regularly, and one American Indian, "The Chief."

We have many women, too. Most of them are called "Sallies" by the others, because they sleep in the dormitories of the Salvation Army on Rivington Street, where they pay forty-five cents a night.

Ours is a great place for nicknames.. The Italians favor special names for each other, such as Joey Fish, who has a seafood pushcart. Another fellow is known as Samson because of his muscles. We have Scotch Mary and Italian Mary and Tommy's Mary; German George and Italian George; Ukrainian Mike and Italian Mike.

No one intends any discrimination because of nationality. We did have tension, however, during World War II, when we had both Chinese and Japanese in the house at the same time. A Japanese woman—an unemployed teacher named Kichi—refused to eat the food served by Chu, the Chinese who was helping us in the kitchen. We had to see to it that she was served separately.

After the bomb was dropped on Hiroshima—"that mortal and unconfessed and unrepented sin" as the diocesan paper of Boston called it—Kichi heard the men in the kitchen say, "The Japs had it coming to them." She began to tremble. For the next year her poor head shook all the while she talked to anyone. Not long after, she died.

We cry out against such names as "Jap" or "Chink" and so on, but we simply have to put up with such familiar nicknames as Italian Mike or Ukrainian Mike. We can only hope that the men themselves don't find them too objectionable.

How many times, all through my life, have I surveyed these tables full of people and wondered if the bread would go around; how many times have I noticed how one heaps his plate and the last one served has little, how one wastes his food and so deprives his brother. German George grumbles as he brings out more sticks of margarine, and refills bread plates, coffeepots, sugar bowls.

Where does it all go? Where do all the people come from? How will it all be paid for? But the miracle is that it does get paid for, sooner or later. The miracle is, also, that seldom do more people come in than we can feed.

Still another miracle for me is the feeling of understanding and friendliness, which must account in large part for the relative order and peace of our home. I was talking the other day to one of the men who used to go to a municipal lodging house nearby, where breakfast and supper are served. "There is always enough food, and thousands are served, but the place is a slaughter house." My friend shuddered. "Many people are afraid to go there. Cops are afraid to interfere—they are not allowed to carry guns. There are gangs who rob every decent person who comes in, and there is no one to stop them. If your clothes are halfway decent, or if your shoes are whole, you lose them. Every night ambulances come to take away people who have been stabbed and beaten."

All during the depression that and other municipal lodging houses were filled, but there was no such violence then, though there were many other complaints about the place. "Why is it that we have the same sort of people coming to us and yet we have no trouble?" I asked him. "In all our thirty years we have had no violence. Just the occasional drunks who get disorderly and rowdy, broken windows, an occasional blow struck." But my friend could see only guns as the solution to the violence of the City Shelter. To me it seemed that fear itself was the cause, and hardly the answer. What continues to surprise me is the way our group does regulate itself. There are injustices, certainly. As St. Paul said, "for they, not knowing the justice of God, seeketh to establish their own." But there is compassion, too, for old-timers, especially, recognize misery when they see it and provide real mutual aid.

One would think that the crowd around the house would thin out after dinner, but they linger on. Strengthened by the food, everyone seems more talkative. Men wait for tobacco. Half a dozen or so wait for "flop money." Some of the women need to be helped out, too.

To me, this is the hardest hour—the evening hour. Then arises the need to discriminate, the need to use common sense, the conflict in trying to follow the Gospel and "to give to him who asks." What to do about the able-bodied who take advantage? How to meet those who drink and have all but exhausted the patience of the people truly trying to forgive seventy times seven? It is easiest when we have literally given away all we have and can say only, "We have no more money."

Charles (when he is not there, Ed takes over) gets through his hard job somehow. At last the crowd thins out with only a few loud talkers still sitting around. Joe Maurer, a late recruit who does just about everything around the place, starts handing out the Compline books. In a good strong voice, the product of Dominican vocal training, he leads us. (He also sings folk songs.) Soon we will drown out the talkers who have grown louder with the advancing hours. More than a dozen young people line up on either side of the clean, decorated dining room table. Joe leads one side, and Michael Kovalak, who was once in a Benedictine monastery and knows the psalm tones, too, leads the other.

"May the Lord Almighty grant us a peaceful night and a perfect end," says Joe.

"Amen," we all reply, fervently.

"Be sober, be watchful," Michael on the other side warns, in the words of St. Peter. "Your adversary the devil, as a roaring lion, goes about seeking someone to devour. Resist him, steadfast in the faith."

As we recite the *confiteor*, I reflect that we, too, have sinned seventy times seven; and how much more than the seven times of the just man have we failed this very day! The absolution brings us the ease to go on with the psalms. The psalm for tonight is the Fifteenth, and it touches my heart:

> I set the Lord ever before me; with him at my right hand
> I shall not be disturbed.
> Therefore my heart is glad and my soul rejoices;
> my body too abides in confidence;
> because you will not abandon my soul to the nether world,
> nor will you suffer your faithful one to undergo corruption.
> You will show me the path to life,
> fullness of joys in your presence,
> delights at your right hand forever.

There is a hymn then, and the little chapter, and responseries, and prayers.

Smokey Joe knows all these by heart—though he is not very tuneful. But then neither are the others. Some sing *basso profundo* and some sing *recto tono*, and if there is an Irish tenor he complicates the sound still more. It does not help matters that two or three older women who are tone deaf delight in singing too. But each enjoys himself, and it is the night prayer of the Church, and God hears. The agnostic sings with the Catholic, because it is a communal act and he loves his brother. Our singing prepares us for another day. Early tomorrow morning the work will start again, and so our life, which St. Teresa of Avila described as a night spent in an uncomfortable inn, resumes. It will continue. The surroundings may be harsh; but where love is, God is.

Marie, who is a Protestant, knows that work is also prayer. During the day she has walked the city streets, gathering up all the newspapers from the refuse baskets on the corners to bring us —this is her contribution to the work of the paper. Now the singing is over. Marie picks up her broom and begins to sweep. Readying the room for tomorrow is her last act of today. She is always the last to leave. When her work is done, she pauses near the door, and then, with a little look-around of satisfaction, departs.

Acknowledgments

Many thanks are due to Edward Sammis, consulting editor, Adrienne Foulke, and William Carter, who rendered invaluable assistance in the preparation of the manuscript and in the location and selection of the photographs.

Photographs

By William Carter: Frontispiece, Pp. 11, 65, 77, 85, 133, 146, 157, 193, 196, 204, 207.

Courtesy Catholic Worker: Pp. 1, 6, 10, 17, 24, 36, 50, 59, 90, 91, 117, 127, 201.

By Vivian Cherry: Pp. 41, 179.

By Mottke Weissman: Pp. 89, 130, 187.

By Robert Lax—*Jubilee:* Pp. 105, 147, 170, 178.

By *U.P.I.:* P. 111.